Floyd
on Africa

KEITH FLOYD

Floyd on Africa

Location Photography by Kim Sayer

Michael Joseph
London

This book is dedicated to the entire crew – especially Sheila Keating
and Scott Rattray – and all of the people who so generously
helped us on our journey (many of whom had never seen a gas stove
or an electric light) and all the cooks out there who do
not give a toss for times, tables, measurements and temperatures.
Cooking is not a science. It is a craft. Like pottery.

STOCKS A number of the recipes in this book use stocks.
Good fresh stocks are available from most supermarkets these days.

MICHAEL JOSEPH LTD

Published by the Penguin Group
27 Wrights Lane, London W8 5TZ
Viking Penguin Inc., 375 Hudson Street, New York, New York 10014, USA
Penguin Books Australia Ltd, Ringwood, Victoria, Australia
Penguin Books Canada Ltd, 10 Alcorn Avenue, Toronto, Ontario, Canada M4V 3B2
Penguin Books (NZ) Ltd, 182-190 Wairau Road, Auckland 10, New Zealand

Penguin Books Ltd, Registered Offices: Harmondsworth, Middlesex, England

First published 1996

1 3 5 7 9 10 8 6 4 2

© Text Floyd on Productions 1996
Location photographs © Floyd on Productions
Recipe food photographer: Steve Baxter
Home economist: Jane Stevenson
Stylist: Roisin Nield
Designer: Janet James

Typeset in Granjon
Colour Reproduction by Radstock Repro, Bath
Printed in England by Butler and Tanner Ltd, Frome, Somerset

A CIP catalogue record for this book is available from the British Library
ISBN 0 7181 4096 6
The moral right of the author has been asserted

Christopher Robin had spent the morning indoors going to Africa
and back...
A. A. Milne, *The House at Pooh Corner*

The Cast

Keith Floyd, Presenter
'Marvellous' Mike Connor, Director
Chris Denham, Producer
Chris Topliss, Camera
Tim White, Sound
Steve Williams, Lighting
Scott Rattray, Floyd's Assistant
Sheila 'Spinoza' Keating, Writer
'Rapid' Kim Sayer, Stills Photographer
Stan 'The Man' Green, Floyd's Manager
Adrian Worsley, Stan Green's Assistant
and Medical Orderly

OF WOKS AND POTJIES AND WONDROUS THINGS

I wanted to call this book *Floyd on Safari*. Or *A Cook's Safari of Africa*. A gastronomic guide to the Dark Continent. But, actually, there isn't any food in Africa. Well, there *is* food in Africa … for the wealthy whites there is the sort of European cuisine that abounded in glossy British magazines of the sixties; for the Africans in the villages and townships there is mealie meal and relish.

And yet the place abounds with exotic produce, and the New South Africa, in particular, is searching valiantly for a new and identifiable cuisine. But in truth I had few memorable meals in hotels or restaurants. And as a cook I was seriously stretched on some parts of my journey to find ingredients, not to mention inspiration. Most of the recipes in this book were created by me on the spur of the moment, guided or manipulated by what was available on the day, and some days there was precious little.

Armed as I was with a converted car wheel, a charcoal stove, a wok and a potjie pot, my options were limited. But, paradoxically, the constraints of these three cooking machines gave me an exhilarating sense of freedom.

Freedom from measurements. Freedom from thermometers and oven temperatures. Freedom from having to tell the cookery editor how many people a leg of kudu or impala can feed – and whether you can get it in Sainsbury's. Or so I thought, for one brief, glorious moment. Cooking by instinct with a handful of this and that over a charcoal fire in the open air has been the most exciting cooking experience of my life. But by the time you read this book you will probably find that my esteemed editor, Louise Haines, has inserted all sorts of things like: 'If you can't find ostrich, use turkey…'

But this book isn't about those sorts of details. This book is about a cooking experience. It is not a text book. It is about a journey. It is about cooking against grandiose backdrops under a Big African Sun. It is not complete. It is not definitive. It is merely a notebook of what cooks do when they spend the day going to Africa.

Creek Lodge, Kinsale, 1996

DAY 4 - 7

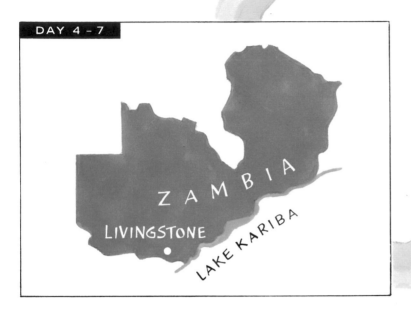

Z A M B I A

LIVINGSTONE

LAKE KARIBA

DA

DAY 1 - 4

ZAMBEZI RIVER

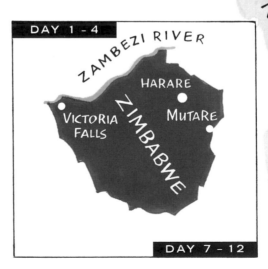

HARARE

VICTORIA
FALLS

ZIMBABWE

MUTARE

DAY 7 - 12

ATLANTIC OCEAN

SO

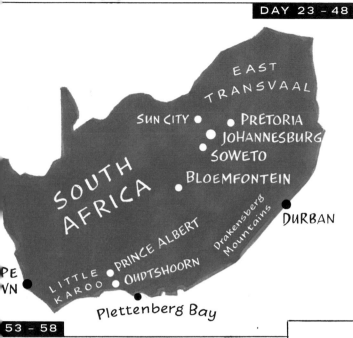

DAY 23 - 48

EAST TRANSVAAL

SUN CITY ● ● PRETORIA
            ● JOHANNESBURG
            ● SOWETO

SOUTH AFRICA

● BLOEMFONTEIN

Drakensberg Mountains

● DURBAN

LITTLE KAROO ● PRINCE ALBERT
            ● OUDTSHOORN

PE
VN

Plettenberg Bay

53 - 58

● MASERU

LESOTHO

DAY 49 - 53

ZAMBIA

ZIMBABWE

Mozambique Channel

MADAGASCAR

INDIAN OCEAN

H AFRICA

LESOTHO

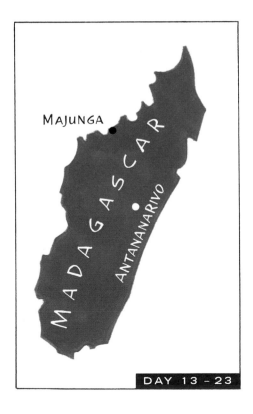

MAJUNGA ●

MADAGASCAR

ANTANANARIVO

DAY 13 - 23

DAY 1

VICTORIA FALLS, ZIMBABWE

The long, straight, newly tarmacked road to Victoria Falls airport cuts through the dust. Here and there baboons amble in the surrounding scrub, past displays of brilliantly painted artefacts and animals carved from wood, attended by smiling ladies in brightly coloured frocks and robes. My manager, Stan, and I are on our way to meet the crew. It is hot, 33°C, rising 38°C, and the air-conditioned Range Rover, ostentatious though it is, is a joy.

The flight from Johannesburg is on time. Everyone seems happy to be reunited – or introduced, as in the case of the new cameraman, Chris, who seems charming, is probably vegetarian and does Tai Chi (this later turns out to be the case). Sheila, who is helping with this book as it must be delivered to the publisher minutes after filming ends, has to be bailed out at immigration. It seems she hasn't been accredited as a member of the crew. We have a new director, Mike, and thankfully Tim (sound) and Steve (lighting), the only remaining chums from the very first *Floyd on...* series, are still with us. I don't believe the programme would be possible without them. My assistant, whose job is to help source and prepare ingredients for the cooking sketches, is Scott Rattray, a young chef from Claridge's. We speak the same language and I am delighted to have him along. Completing the team is photographer Kim Sayer, who will be taking the stills for this book. Oh, and of course, Adrian Worsley, who comes from Cumbria and has been, among other things, a male nurse and a prison officer. He should be very useful.

The usual elation at the prospect of the job ahead is somewhat dashed by the absence of several important cases: notably half of Steve's lighting kit, Chris's lens filters, bits of Tim's sound equipment and almost all of Kim's cameras. The inevitable form-filling and cross-checking begins ...

The Victoria Falls Safari Lodge aims to look like a tree-house. It is a cheerful-looking wooden construction, vividly painted and tiled, with a steeply thatched roof that blends in with the buff-coloured scrub around. Directly below us is a large waterhole. The hotel has been built principally for those who want to watch wildlife, and the waterhole, of course, attracts them. It is our job – hopefully – to film them. The crew seem eager and ready for action despite the long flight and depleted equipment. After a few of the local Zambezi beers and a spot of lunch we head off into the bush, in search of animals.

Ray Stocker, our Zimbabwean guide, and a former officer in both the Rhodesian and Zimbabwean armies, is neat in his khaki drills and wide-brimmed hat. He has the relaxed attitude of a man who has spent a long time in the bush. It is hot, dusty and uncomfortable in the open vehicles. We see no animals. Disappointed, we return to the hotel.

Little by little, as dusk begins to fall, they come. First the birds: a Cape turtle dove and a pied kingfisher, circling above the waterhole. Then, tentatively, the kudu come to drink. They are elegant and graceful antelopes with a band of distinguishing stripes on their flanks. The males have tall horns. Finally, half-a-dozen huge grey shadows emerge from the thickets. They are elephants. It seems as though they are on tiptoe. They make no sound.

First they draw up water through their trunks, squirting it into their mouths. When they have drunk their fill they suck up dust and sand and give themselves a mud bath. Then as quietly as they came they retreat into the deepening gloom of the African night.

DAY 2

CHINOTIMBA ROAD

In the half-light just before dawn I awake eagerly and step out on to the balcony of my room. The waterhole is deserted. At breakfast time the crew return from an early morning sortie with Ray in search of animals. They haven't found so much as a cat.

The first cooking sketch of the series is to be filmed by the waterhole this evening. We hope that the elephants will arrive to provide the backdrop. I set out with Scott and the film crew to visit the market in the township, to find some local ingredients for my dish. I have decided to make a bush hunter's stew with kudu and warthog, a kind of wild pig.

The town of Victoria Falls is like a cross between a frontier post (indeed it is opposite the Zambian border) and the beginnings of a resort. Luxurious new houses are in a state of semi-construction, next to simple concrete buildings that house gift shops, travel agents and white-water-rafting and safari-trip offices. There appears to be no bar, just a couple of hotels and a profusion of safari vehicles. The centre of activity seems to be the Wimpy Bar. I see no evidence of any kind of local food being served or sold. Someone says we will find what we are looking for at the township, where, alongside the market, the locals eat and drink the local beer at the Chinotimba Beer Hall on Chinotimba Road.

The township is about five minutes from the centre of Victoria Falls, where some 2,000 white people operate their businesses. The township houses around 28,000 black people in dwellings spread over many miles, offering various descending degrees of comfort, from breeze block cabins to simple mud huts with straw roofs. Around the houses the tawny-coloured earth, which sometimes shades into ochre or burnt sienna, is broken up by vivid evergreens and startling scarlet, pink and purple bougainvillea. As well as the market and the beer hall, there is a school and a clinic.

At the market alongside the Chinotimba Beer Hall, Victoria Falls

12

The market is vibrant and alive with happy faces and the sound of laughter. The stalls, though they all sell similar produce, are stocked plentifully, and the stallholders are eager to join in the fun that the appearance of the film crew seems to be creating. Children scamper behind and in front of us and large, multicoloured ladies grasp me in bearhugs and beam for the camera. Others, some with smiling babies bound to their backs with scarves or towels, watch intrigued. It is a happy occasion and though everybody seems to be surprised to see our white faces, they make us very welcome. Our town guide, who shall remain nameless, confesses it is the first time he has visited the township. It is an omission which is to become something of a recurrent theme throughout our journey.

Under drapes of sacking erected against the heat of the late morning sun there are mounds of bananas, tomatoes and sweet potatoes and bowls of rape greens, pumpkin greens or cassava (yam) greens. Cardboard boxes are filled with dried greens and tomatoes. These will be vital when the rains come, from about November to February, and fresh vegetables are scarce. There are sacks of nuts, seeds and ground maize, bowls of dried caterpillars and dried tiger fish and kapenta (which resemble whitebait, but are, in fact, tiny sardines that taste rather like Bombay duck) from the Zambezi River. Frankly, the kapenta and caterpillars would be better off left in the Zambezi and the trees whence they came.

One stall is piled high with enormous bales of locally grown tobacco, selling for 5 Zimbabwe dollars – known as Zimdollars – a bundle (less than 50 pence). It is intended for smoking in pipes. I am reminded of my days as a sixteen-year-old working at the bonded warehouse of W. D. & H. O. Wills, makers of Woodbines, in Bristol. Taking aside five-foot barrels packed with tobacco, while a crane lifted off the top, inserted a great spike into the middle of the bales and drew out a piece for the customs officer to inspect.

One section of the market is devoted to craftsmen dealing in tin, corrugated iron and steel. Here they will hammer and fashion anything from cooking pans to tin baths or money-boxes. We negotiate the fabrication of two tin trunks to house the cooking equipment for our trip. They will, the craftsman says, be ready by 2 p.m. tomorrow. They will cost 200 Zimdollars, approximately £18. A good deal.

Next to the market is a large concrete compound, rather like a disused cattle market. Inside are long trestle benches and tables where men and a few women sit quaffing a thick, foaming, creamy pink alcoholic drink they call beer (or chibuku) from huge plastic buckets. Outside the beer hall is a tractor. Behind it is a stainless steel tanker used to deliver the chibuku, which is made from maize, a local crop called sorghum, and yeast. It is transferred to

TOP: Hands of tobacco

ABOVE: A refreshing slurp

stainless steel tanks above the beer hall and, while still fermenting, it is pumped through archaic-looking serving vessels below into two- or four-litre containers. At high times some 4,000–6,000 litres of beer are sold here a day.

Across the compound are three simple stalls, where large black ladies stir large black pots over wood fires. It is time for lunch. The local diet revolves around mealie: maize boiled up with water until it makes a thick porridge, called sadza, which is rather like polenta or stiff mashed potato. It is worked with the fingers into balls and used to scoop up the relish (the generic name for whatever vegetables or meat are served with it, and without which the mealie would be virtually tasteless). Usually there are greens, cooked in a pan without water and mixed with tomatoes, onions or garlic. Sometimes they are sprinkled with ground peanuts or the kapenta fish, fried in oil. The dried caterpillars can also be fried and ground up as a seasoning. I pay 7 Zimdollars and am given a plate of stewed beef, greens and mealie. It is the best meal I have eaten since I arrived in Africa.

Kim, a gentle, charming man, who frequently gets lost in a photographic world of his own, is captivated by the colour and characters. We almost leave without him. This would also become a recurring situation.

There is one more port of call. The local supermarket, run by a bubbly Indian lady. It is a terrific haphazard bazaar in which shelves and boxes are stacked and packed higgledy-piggledy fashion with enamel saucepans circa 1950, bars of Lifebuoy soap, tins of condensed milk, plastic buckets, mops, dried fish and packets of Jacob's Cream Crackers. I spend a Zimbabwean fortune buying black enamelled cooking pots for no other reason than that they remind me of my grandmother's kitchen.

ABOUT MEALIE

- Portuguese traders introduced maize originally to the east coast of Africa. They called it milho, which the Voortrekkers (the Dutch families who made the Great Trek from the Cape to the interior) called mielie – mealie in English.

- It is the staple diet of African people throughout the continent. In country areas the corn is still pounded into flour by hand on grinding stones or with enormous pestles and mortars. It is then mixed with water and cooked to make a porridge, which is sometimes called mealie meal, sometimes mealie pap. In Zimbabwe it is known as sadza, in Zambia nshima, and in Lesotho papa. It is served with whatever stewed vegetables or meat are available.

- In different regions and among different tribes the consistency of the mealie porridge varies from soft and moist to dry and crumbly.

Later. Waterhole number two, somewhere in the Zimbabwean bush

The Range Rover and Long Wheel Base Land Rover Defender are loaded with cooking equipment, food and my very special ice-box containing Mars bars and dark chocolate, mineral water, whisky and apples. A flight has arrived at Victoria Falls airport carrying Kim's cameras and some – but not all – of the missing filming equipment. The inquiries continue.

Nothing is stirring at the waterhole below our hotel, so we head off with enthusiasm for waterhole number two at Kalisosa Vlei, deeper into the bush, where, says Ray, the elephants will come at dusk.

Twenty-five kilometres down a corrugated mud road a slippery, shiny sand track leads into the bush proper. The waterhole glistens in the bright high sun of the afternoon. There are heaps of dung and the trees have been brutalized by hungry animals. The elephants cannot be far away.

The waterholes are man-made and pumped daily with water. Apart from quenching the animals' thirst, the waterholes help to spread the game out, preventing large herds of buffalo and elephant from congregating along the river and gradually destroying the vegetation along its fringe. Left to themselves the elephants would make their own waterholes in old salt-lakes and places which trap rainwater, digging deeper and deeper as they shower themselves with mud until, eventually, with good rains, the waterholes become perennial. But last year the rains stopped short. The Zambezi is at its lowest for almost forty-five years, and in areas where there are no man-made waterholes and little surviving vegetation, animals will inevitably be lost.

Despite the drought, there are still bands of virulent evergreens, but in the curious way of the world, although they are strong and sturdy, their leaves are pointed and contain an unpleasant liquor which precludes the animals from eating them.

It is a tense day for me. I am to cook with a new director and cameraman. While I set about making a fire, the crew put up lights and unload reflectors, sound equipment and all the paraphernalia that goes with filming. A brightly coloured ex-British army Bedford truck grinds past, laden with curious locals who wave and grin and cheer. We look like a circus. I wonder what the elephants will make of us. If they come. Despite Ray's laid back demeanour, he has propped a 4.485 rifle within easy reach. It is loaded.

I am to cook my hunter's stew in a Dutch oven, one of the black cast-iron pots known as potjies. They have tight-fitting lids and three little legs which can be set into the coals once the flames of the fire have died down. The trick is to scrape and bank the coals around the pot to provide all-round heating. The slowly cooked meat and vegetables cooked in these pots, first introduced by Dutch pioneers in the seventeenth century, can be quite delicious.

I propose to cook the kudu and warthog with a marmalade of onions and tomatoes, chunks of carrot, celery, some local red wine and finally some mushrooms and delicious indigenous butternut squash. Mike, the director, says, 'Action', Chris, the cameraman, says, 'Speed'. I launch into the sequence. For a first take it is impeccable in every way, except that I get the country wrong. 'Here we are in Zambia…' I make it worse by referring to the local wine as a light Zambian red. We have to go again.

Fortunately, Scott has prepared three sets of raw ingredients, so it is a matter of seconds before the cooking-pot is emptied and we begin over. This time I get the country right, but the Mukuyu Gallery 94 Renaissance dry Zimbabwean red wine still defeats me. No one seems angry, dismayed or distressed. The atmosphere is very jolly for new hands on a first day. Eventually I get it all right and the dish is ready. A moody shot is set up at a table in the bush as the sun begins to sink like a stone and the skeletal trees stand out

starkly against the sky. I put a plate of stew in front of Ray and ask: 'What is it like living in the bush?' He sits back, his hat brim bent down over his blue eyes, and squinting back at me he says laconically: 'It's hot.'

As if in a Graham Greene or Somerset Maugham novel we drink sundowners. The gin seems part of the scene at dusk in Africa. The sun finally sinks behind the vehicles, as we wait and hope for the elephants. There are no elephants.

Later, while chatting at the bar of the hotel, I appear to collapse with a blinding migraine. The paramedics arrive in flashing vans and carry me away, ha-ha. The efficient, smiling, quiet-mannered doctor gives me an injection and pills and I am back on track.

Hunter's Stew

Serves 4

450g (1lb) warthog or leg or
    shoulder of pork
450g (1lb) kudu or venison
vegetable oil
salt and freshly ground black
    pepper
4 onions, finely chopped
700g (1½lb) tomatoes, skinned,
    seeded and diced

¾ bottle of fruity red wine
3 sticks of celery, cut into 5cm
    (2in) chunks
4 large carrots, cut into 5cm (2in)
    chunks
275g (10oz) butternut squash or
    pumpkin
225g (8oz) mushrooms, sliced

Cut all the meat into hefty chunks, about 5 x 5cm (2 x 2in). Heat the oil in a flameproof casserole or large saucepan and seal the meat quickly. Lift out the meat, season and reserve.

Put the onions into the same pot and allow to sweat gently for 5–10 minutes until soft but not coloured. Add the tomatoes and cook for a few minutes.

Return the meat to the pot, stir in the wine, bring to the boil, then turn down the heat to a simmer. Cook, covered, for 1 hour, then add the celery and carrots and continue to simmer for a further 1½ hours until the meat is tender. Twenty minutes before the end of the cooking time, add the squash or pumpkin, then 10 minutes before the end, stir in the mushrooms.

PLEASE NOTE

All measurements, cooking times and oven temperatures are given as a rough guide only. Remember that scales and ovens vary and ingredients are never exactly the same. A dish is only cooked when you are satisfied and not when the recipe says it should be.

DAY 3

SOMEWHERE BEGINNING WITH Z

Morning at the waterhole and fifty buffalo are gathered. Earlier there have been warthogs and a few kudu. A flurry of small animals comes rushing and scrambling up the scrubby bank below to drink at a tiny pool. They look like baby armadillos, but they are banded mongooses. The crew return from another early morning drive in search of animals. They have drawn a blank again. As they approach, the mongooses scurry back down the hill and one by one the buffalo pick themselves up and shamble off to pastures further away.

We are off to see the Falls, one of the seven wonders of the modern world. Along the Zambezi much of the National Park is fenced off with barbed wire. It is peppered with mines from the guerrilla war against Rhodesia. They have killed many animals, but so far no human beings. Close to the road there are enormous baobab trees, some maybe 3,000 years old. According to tribal legend God was in a rage one day so he ripped up the baobabs and planted them upside down. In Australia they are known as boab trees and the Aboriginals tell the same story. Here, they say that the white blossoms are supposed to be inhabited by spirits, and anyone who picks them will be eaten by a lion. A piece of information which may come in jolly useful later.

At this point, there will be a pause for a quick history and geography lesson on the subject of the Victoria Falls. On the morning of 16 November 1855, the Scottish explorer David Livingstone, on a mission to open up the Zambezi River into 'God's Highway', bringing European goods to the natives, first heard the roar of the spectacle the local people called 'the smoke that thunders'. In his small canoe he and his party of oarsmen arrived at what is now Livingstone Island at the very edge of this great natural phenomenon, caused by the gradual eroding action

From my hotel window: a man-made oasis for animals in a country desperate for rain of massive amounts of fast-flowing water. Later Livingstone wrote: 'Scenes so lovely must have been gazed upon by angels in their flight.' He declared that the mile-wide curtain of water should be known as the Victoria Falls in honour of the Queen of England.

I find myself twisting the words to the old Sinatra song: 'Let's all go to Victoria. Next time we'll look at the Falls...' With impeccable timing the *Floyd on Africa* crew have arrived when the Falls are, comparatively speaking, a trickle, due to the lack of water in the Zambezi. Even though they are not the spectacle they might be, they are still terribly frightening.

At the viewpoint known as the Devil's Cataract, one section of the Falls still rushes and thunders, crowned by the famous rainbow which appears in the early afternoon. My director would like me to stand at the very edge, gesticulating enthusiastically for the cameras. I politely decline to go anywhere near the brink of the stomach-churning chasm opening up below me. As gorges go I would be far happier at Cheddar.

In my piece to camera, at a safe distance from the edge, the curse of the Z words strikes again. Am I in Zambia or Zimbabwe? We decide to redraw the map of Africa to show 'Zimbambwezi', an area known by television presenters to include Zambia, Zimbabwe and the Zambezi River.

Victoria Falls

Back at the hotel inside my luxurious, two-floored suite something is amiss. The fruit basket lies upended on the floor, melon peel litters the stairs, boxes of films have been tampered with and the little good-night chocolates I had been saving up for a midnight feast have been eaten through their cardboard packets.

I creep cautiously about the apartment, looking for the perpetrators of the crime. Even my manager, Stan, would surely have taken the chocolates out of their boxes before eating them.

There is no one there, but the windows are open, and there are small prints in the dust. The monkeys have been to visit.

THE GUIDE'S TALE

Ray Stocker has been a canoe/safari guide for twelve years.

'I've only ever lived in a city for about eight months, and then I got ill,' says Ray Stocker. 'I was raised on a farm, and I love the wild. I think everybody has a bit of the old hunter-gatherer blood in them – just some people have more than others. Deep down I believe most people would rather live this sort of life than the kind they actually live.

'It's very interesting to watch people's reactions when they go into the bush for the first time. Some don't believe there is any danger whatsoever and happily go up to an elephant and feed it with an apple. Others get very, very nervous at even the sight of one a long way away. Our job is to control that mixture of bravery and fear. On the longer trips people really see a facet of the world that they have never been aware of, and nine times out of ten they come back.

'Every animal has its own social set-up – for example, elephants have a matriarchal society, in which the fully-grown males are only allowed to be part of the herd for the four weeks of

I think this is the chap who stole my chocolates

the breeding season. Then they are chased off. Young bulls live with the females until they reach about twelve to fifteen years old and then they are thrown out to join the other males. It is quite a sad thing to see, because they want to stay with mum. With lions it is very different. You will find a dominant male with a group of lionesses. If there is any change in the dominant male, the newcomer will usually kill off all the cubs, and then establish his own line.

'The animals are seldom dangerous – as long as you know how to deal with them. I have only been bitten by a lion once. We were sleeping in the open around a fire. It was moonlit and about three o'clock in the morning when I felt something thrashing around. I opened my eyes to see four lions treading my sleeping-bag. I was carrying a 44 Magnum and I jumped up and started shouting at them and they pushed off. With most animals in this situation you should never run, but you need to act aggressively – they respect another "animal" who is holding his own territory. If you have ever played with a kitten on the carpet you will notice that if you run your finger away from it, it will give chase. If you push your hand towards it it will back off. It's exactly the same with a bigger cat.

'We have a few incidents every year of crocodiles attacking people on the banks of the Zambezi. On one occasion some poachers came into my camp at night and I chased them off into the river. One of them was eaten by a croc. Fortunately we've only had one instance canoeing, when a guide had one leg eaten by a crocodile. The kayaks we use often get bitten – but the trick is not to get tipped overboard, or to get upturned by a hippo.

'Snakes are rarely as dangerous as people think. Mostly they are shy and when they hear you coming, they get out of the way. If you respect them and don't try to grab them, they won't hurt you. However we do have one, the puff adder, which I reckon is the most dangerous of them all, because it is very slow-moving and can't get out of your way. So try not to step on one!'

ABOUT ELEPHANTS

- Elephants need to take in about 100 litres of water per fully-grown animal every twenty-four hours.
- An adult elephant will remove about 5 tonnes of mud from various waterholes every year in the ritual of the mud bath.
- They like clean water, unlike buffalo, which like muddy water.
- Elephants' life-spans are similar to those of human beings. Sometimes they live to be ninety.
- They have six sets of teeth in their lifetime. When they lose their last set they die, as they are unable to feed properly.
- An adult eats about 250 kilos of food a day: mostly branches, bark, grasses, roots and fruit. The acacia is a great delicacy.

DAY 4

ZAMBIA

In Africa the pace is set by the oxen.
(*Local saying*)

The bureaucracy at the border between Zambia and Zimbabwe is bewildering, archaic and funny. I have visited few countries in which the officials are so happy, friendly and helpful, even though the piece of paper they issued to you yesterday is invalid today, and the one you thought you ought to have had in the first place is now required. The process is slow, but gradually we are adjusting to the pace of life in Africa.

The two customs buildings, one on each side of the border, are drab concrete affairs that inside have the air of derelict classrooms. Some of the walls are painted in a lurid gloss green, others have simple, colourful murals depicting the attractions of the area. There are handwritten official notices warning against itinerant money-changers or reminding you to be sure to obtain a receipt for any moneys handed over to an official. I wonder why.

Outside Scott has left the window of the Defender open and a monkey is sitting at the steering-wheel.

We head across no-man's-land towards the Victoria Falls Bridge, which links the two countries. In 1975 Ian Smith, B. J. Vorster, Kenneth Kaunda, Abel Muzorewa and Joshua Nkomo met in a railway carriage parked on the bridge to discuss the future of Zimbabwe. Today, half-way across the bridge, a group of lunatics are cheerfully bungee jumping. At 110 metres they say this is the highest/longest/tallest commercial jump in the world. It's funny, everywhere I go they always have the highest tide in the world, the largest waterfall in the world and, of course, the highest/longest/tallest commercial jump in the world.

The bush on the Zambian side of the border looks very much like that on the Zimbabwean side, and yet there is an almost tangible difference between the two countries. Zambia has only 8 million population (Zimbabwe has 11 million) and is incredibly poor. But the people are extremely friendly, relaxed and appear to be happy. Livingstone, the former capital of Northern Rhodesia, was once a model colonial town. Now it is a run-down shambles where the street lights don't work and the roads are full of potholes.

The nearby Dambwa Market, however, is a much bigger and more bustling affair than its counterpart in the township at Victoria Falls. Covered concrete stalls built in a square sell a profusion of goods from stationery to lipstick, floor polish, bars of soap, bags of sugar and perm lotion. I wonder about the perm lotion.

Crossing into Zambia at speed and in great comfort

Scenes from a Zambian market

In the centre of the square are open stalls, laden with vegetables and fruits, and stoves where the ubiquitous pots of mealie (known here as nshima), stew and greens are cooking. A young woman with a tiny baby strapped to her back sells pieces of fried chicken which she spears from a pot. Another woman is frying doughnuts. Children sell cold drinks from coolboxes.

Outside more traders sell sacks of mealie and salt. There are mounds of grains and nuts. Cabbages peep out from under sacking and there are heaps of wild muchenje fruit, known as African biscuit because of their thick, dry, crumbly pith. Inside they have soft, sweet, kidney-shaped fruit.

A long, undulating, straight road leads from Livingstone to Tongabezi Lodge. Baboons scamper across the road and in the distance the occasional elephant crunches through the bush. Women carrying bundles on their heads walk by the roadside, and groups of uniformed children carry rucksacks to school. There are makeshift stalls by the roadside where scrawny carcasses and cuts of meat hang on simple frameworks cut from trees. We pull up at a small, concrete, flat-roofed edifice that calls itself a restaurant. It serves Coca-Cola and samosas.

Tongabezi Lodge, on the banks of the Zambezi, is clearly someone's fantasy. It consists of a three-sided library/lounge/bar and several 'rooms' which are, in fact, tents within wooden structures and with thatched roofs. Built high into the cliff is the elegant honeymoon suite, with its sunken bath and four-poster bed. It, too, is open-fronted. The clientele appear to be those who, if they don't actually play polo, certainly watch it, are probably members of the Hurlingham Club and always manage to get centre court tickets at Wimbledon.

Scottish chef Craig Higgins has masterminded a lush kitchen garden full of vegetables and herbs, and when the sun sets only the chatter of the guests dining by candlelight in the open air and the soft rhythmic voices of the Tongabezi Staff Choir disturb the tranquillity and total isolation. Co-owner Ben Parker is a charming, diffident guy, who promises to introduce me to a genuine, non-tourist fishing village called Lioka, further down the Zambezi. But first, I must cook dinner at Tongabezi.

Tongabezi Chicken Curry

Serves 4

2 sweet potatoes

1 butternut squash

4 large chicken joints, halved

salt and freshly ground black
  pepper

vegetable oil

2 onions, finely chopped

2 tomatoes, skinned, seeded and
  diced

2 garlic cloves, finely chopped

15g (½oz) fresh root ginger,
  finely chopped

6 cardamom seeds

1 heaped teaspoon curry powder

450ml (¾ pint) chicken stock

2 sticks lemon grass, bruised

2 small red chillies, finely
  chopped

300ml (½ pint) yogurt

1 tablespoon finely chopped fresh
  coriander

Parboil the sweet potatoes in their skins for about 10 minutes, then peel and cut into thick slices. Cut the squash into similar-sized pieces.

Season the chicken pieces. Heat some vegetable oil in a large pan and fry the chicken for about 15 minutes until golden. Remove from the pan and keep warm. Add the onions to the pan and cook gently until soft, then add the tomatoes, garlic, ginger, cardamom and curry powder and cook for a few minutes. Return the chicken to the pan, add the stock and lemon grass, then cover and simmer for about 10 minutes, or until the chicken is cooked through.

Meanwhile, heat a little more vegetable oil in another pan and fry the pieces of sweet potato and squash over a medium heat for about 10 minutes until slightly golden and crispy on the outside and soft on the inside. Keep warm.

When the chicken is cooked, add the chopped chillies to the pan and cook for 2 minutes or so. Stir in the yogurt and heat through without boiling. Sprinkle with chopped coriander and serve with the sautéed sweet potatoes and squash.

DAY 5

LIOKA FISHING VILLAGE

Let fools build and clever ones destroy.
(*Painted on a mud hut in Lioka fishing village*)

Officially the village of Lioka has only seventy-four inhabitants but at least 200 people greet us when we arrive. The children come rushing and skipping, young bucks stand around in knots, chatting jauntily. The women at first appear more shy, but gradually emerge, laughing. Many are wearing their finest clothes and lipstick. I sense there is someone missing. Kim has been so busy taking photographs that he has been left behind in Tongabezi. A canoe is dispatched to rescue him.

In Zambia alone there are some seventy-three dialects. In some areas communities only 100 kilometres apart have difficulty understanding one another. Here they speak Tokaleya, a mixture of Tonga and Lozi, but as is the case everywhere in Africa, for those who have been to school, English is the common (and official) language.

The villagers make their living from fishing. Men in teams of four work with nets and dug-out canoes. Some of the fish they sell, the rest they eat. They also keep cattle that provide meat and milk. Their houses are simple affairs. One woman is single-handedly building an extra room, packing mud into a wooden frame. It will take two to three days to bake and dry out in the sun. Many of the huts are charmingly decorated with patterns and words of wisdom,

BELOW RIGHT: She doesn't think it outrageous that she's building the house while her husband philosophises over home-brewed beer

using dyes made from ochre, sienna or black earth mixed with water.

A group of women make cooking oil. Using a stone and small hammer, they crack open the shells from the wild bush nuts called mangongo (like groundnuts), then they pound the kernels in an enormous mungo and nchili (pestle and mortar), fashioned from a tree. The nuts are boiled for a long time until the oil floats to the top, then it is skimmed off and boiled up a second time.

Some of the oil will be used to baste the whole pig I am to roast over a wood fire. It has been scored on the outside and stuffed with a whole celery, halved onions, lemons and crushed cloves of garlic. We erect the spit, made to Stan's design, at the Victoria Falls township market and light a wood fire. As I pour a gallon of paraffin over the stacked branches Tim makes the observation: 'An African makes a small fire and sits close to it. An Englishman lights a large fire and stands away from it.'

The pig takes six hours to roast and in the heat of the afternoon the village drummers begin to tap out a rhythm, the women to sway and sing. Much later as we set off into the dusk the sound of music and laughter is still ringing out joyfully through the bush.

ABOVE: Making mealie meal

DAY 6

LIVINGSTONE ISLAND, I PRESUME

Like Christopher Robin, I have spent the morning going to Zambia and Zimbabwe and back. The quaint proceedings are still bewildering. Sometimes the first official gives you a piece of ripped-off paper with your car registration and the number of occupants written on it. It is essential that you give it to the officer at the next booth along. At other times you are not given the paper and are sent back to get it. Adrian is pulled in and body-searched for drugs. He declares ten weeks' supply of malaria pills.

The journey by canoe over mini-rapids to Livingstone Island, on the edge of the Falls, on the Zambian side, is an exhilarating one. Waiting for the crew boat to move into position for filming, I cast my line and hook and land a splendid tiger fish. Chris lets the camera run. In more than ten years of filming, the *Floyd on...* series has established a fine record of losing fish on camera, so I am feeling rather pleased with myself.

No washday blues here

On the island I cook my fish with cabbage African-style on the very edge of the Falls. Everything is going swimmingly and everyone is allowed to make one joke containing the words 'I presume'.

Tiger Fish with Spring Greens, Tomato, Onions and Garlic

Your local supermarket will not sell tiger fish; substitute any fillets of white fish, for example sole or bream.

Serves 2

100g (4oz) butter, plus a little for frying the fish

½ medium onion, very finely chopped

4 plum tomatoes, skinned, seeded and diced

2 garlic cloves, finely chopped

450g (1lb) spring cabbage, chard, rape greens or spinach, very finely chopped

400g (14oz) fish fillets

2 tablespoons lemon juice

1 level dessertspoon chopped fresh parsley

1 tablespoon ground fresh nuts, for example, peanuts, almonds, walnuts, etc. (optional)

lemon wedges, to garnish

Melt half the butter in a pan and sauté the onion and tomatoes for a few minutes until soft. Add the garlic and cabbage, cover the pan, and cook over a low heat for about 6 minutes until tender, checking and stirring from time to time.

Meanwhile, heat a knob of butter in a pan and quickly fry the fish fillets on both sides until golden. Remove from the pan and keep warm.

Wipe out the pan, put in the remaining butter, and cook for a few moments until golden. Stir in the lemon juice and parsley, heat through and pour over the fish. Garnish with the nuts and lemon wedges.

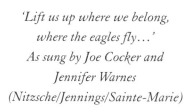

'Lift us up where we belong,
where the eagles fly…'
As sung by Joe Cocker and
Jennifer Warnes
(Nitzsche/Jennings/Sainte-Marie)

Hot and dusty, I take a bush shower from a bucket suspended from a tree. Refreshed, I swallow my fears, take a deep breath and allow myself to be whisked away in a microlite for a breathtaking flight over the Falls. Mike, the pilot, explains that the site of the Falls is shifting further and further back due to the powerful flow of water. From this eagle's viewpoint I can clearly see the place where they originally formed. What lyrical prose would Dr Livingstone have summoned had he been able to enjoy this view, I wonder?

Where eagles dare …

At 3 p.m. we wrap and I return to the hotel. At 6 p.m. the crew arrive hot, angry, tired and dehydrated. We have cocked up the travel arrangements. In the heat of the afternoon and with the day's supply of water finished, Tim, Chris and Kim have been forced to ride on the roof-rack of the sole Land Rover, already laden with the rest of the crew and equipment. At the border the police have stopped them and made them return to the hotel by taxi.

The night's management meeting begins somewhat acrimoniously, but guilt is admitted, apologies accepted and there are drinks all round. A new system is in place. This will not happen again.

Victoria Falls from
Livingstone Island, Zambia

DAY 7

GOODBYE VICTORIA FALLS

Today we leave Victoria Falls for the Leopard Rock Hotel, perched on 'The Hill of Tired Feet' in the Eastern Highlands of Zimbabwe. For a new crew we seem to be settling down extremely well, despite last night's mishap. Chris the cameraman is fearless – happy to sit on the precipitous edge of the Falls or film from a microlite. The director, Mike, has a boundless (he would say marvellous) energy and enthusiasm for the project and Tim and Steve are proving once again what stalwart members of the crew they are.

As for me, they say that in the bush, a man needs a keen eye, a sharp sense of changing weather and years of experience to recognize the marks and spores of the creatures who may be nearby. But after only a few days I can now recognize, in an instant, the imprint of an Adidas trainer-wearing cameraman and the tracks of an Abercrombie & Kent safari truck.

There is still no news of the remaining missing equipment. We must leave without it. As we are about to go, 350 buffalo turn up at the waterhole to say goodbye. The crew hastily unpack their cameras and capture them on film. At last. Marvellous, says Mike.

After the sweltering heat of the last week I have repacked my six suitcases for the journey to Leopard Rock. My contingency woolly jumpers, heavy jackets and wellies are stowed away at the bottom of the luggage. I don't expect to need them again until we return to London in November.

The crew depart from Harare airport in a minibus for the five-hour drive to Leopard Rock. I am to spend the night at the Imba Matombo Lodge, which means House of Stone. It is an elegant country house in the hills about fifteen kilometres from Harare with a tall, pointed, beautifully thatched roof and little rotund bungalows. Tomorrow I will fly into Leopard Rock by light aircraft.

Drinks are served in the drawing-room by the butler, a splendidly formal Zimbabwean, dapper in his crisp white shirt, black silk bow tie and cummerbund. Dinner is taken on the fine old polished wood table with silver candelabra and gorgeous flowers. It is a splendidly simple affair of creamy, lightly curried, spicy pumpkin and apple soup, followed by Zimbabwean lamb with a light rosemary-flavoured gravy, a purée of fresh sweet carrots, perfectly roasted potatoes and finely presented spinach. For pudding I have a crisp chocolate biscuit with pecan nut chocolate cream, set in a lake of rich dark chocolate sauce.

In the drawing-room, waiting for coffee and brandy, the now nightly migraine strikes. Tired of taking the tablets, I march up and down the immaculately manicured lawn outside the lodge for twenty minutes, swinging my arms shoulder-high, taking deep breaths. No doubt everyone thinks I have gone barking mad. But it works. I knock back the migraine and retire to my gaily decorated room, rich with brightly coloured tapestries, rugs and hand-painted papier-mâché animals. I sleep like a baby. This turns out to be the last migraine of the trip.

Lightly Curried Pumpkin and Apple Soup

This excellent soup was served to me at the Imba Matombo Lodge, near Harare.

Serves 4

25ml (1fl oz) sunflower oil

15g (½oz) butter

1 large onion, chopped

450g (1lb) butternut squash, peeled and cubed

200g (7oz) peeled and cubed potato

2 medium eating apples, peeled and cubed

½ teaspoon ground turmeric

1 teaspoon curry powder

½ teaspoon ground cinnamon

½ teaspoon ground ginger

750ml (1¼ pints) chicken stock

½ teaspoon salt

1 bay leaf

small pinch of sugar

100ml (4fl oz) milk

25ml (1fl oz) brandy

To serve:

whipped or soured cream

a little paprika or 1 tablespoon chopped fresh chives

Heat the oil and butter in a large pan, add the onion and sauté until golden. Add the squash, potato, apples and spices and toss together over a low heat for about 2 minutes, until the fruit and vegetables are coated and the aromas of the spices are released. Add the stock, salt, bay leaf and sugar, bring to the boil, cover and simmer gently for about 25 minutes until the vegetables are soft.

Cool until lukewarm, then remove the bay leaf. Purée the soup in a blender until absolutely smooth. Reheat gently in a clean pan, adding just enough milk to give a medium-thick consistency. Add the brandy and heat through without boiling. Ladle the soup into warmed bowls, top each one with a little cream and dust with paprika or sprinkle with chopped chives.

DAY 8

HARARE AIRPORT

It is 5 a.m. and the weather has closed in. The six-seater Piper Navajo aircraft waits on the runway, destination Mutare airport in the Eastern Highlands of Zimbabwe. But we cannot land at Mutare. Visibility is nil and the temperature has dropped to 14°C. Two hours later we are given the all-clear to take off, but the filthy weather at Mutare is relentless. The light aircraft is diverted to a military airport called Grand Reef, much to the consternation of the one reluctant hero in his combat gear who is there to guard it.

At the Leopard Rock Hotel Mike is pacing up and down waiting to film my arrival. There is no news. He is told that at Mutare there is a 'ticky' phone by the airstrip, which the public can use to get up-to-date flight information. He and the crew pile into their minibus and race off to the airstrip. Someone has stolen the ticky phone in the night. Finally a message gets through that I have landed elsewhere and Kim comes to the rescue in the Land Rover.

Some say Leopard Rock is so called because leopards once basked here, some say it is because the rock at the top of the mountain is shaped like a leopard. The Queen Mother is quoted as saying there is nowhere more beautiful in Africa. The hotel has its own coffee plantation and in the fertile hills and valleys tobacco, bananas, lychees and mangoes are grown. But I can see nothing. The Hill of Tired Feet is wrapped in a cotton-wool ball of mist. Coming in from the chilly morning air I find myself shivering. A waiter called Jealous brings me a cup of steaming hot chocolate.

DAY 9

THE BURMA VALLEY

In the night there have been storms. The bush fire which last night was snaking up the valley is out, but the electricity has gone down and emergency generators have taken over. Leopard Rock is like the Quantocks in mid-November. Though the weather is a shock, I have to admit that it is quite refreshing after the intense arid heat of the bush. And the area badly needs rain. In the hotel bedrooms are notes suggesting that shared baths help save water, but Adrian has a moustache and Stan has been eating too much junk food, and I don't think we'd fit.

Armed with umbrellas and jackets we set off to cook at the banana plantation village in the Burma Valley below Leopard Rock. Through the swirls of mist I begin to make out shapes as the road twists its way down the mountain. The shapes materialize into long-haired monkeys. As the mist clears I can see gorgeous colours: burnt sienna and ochre earth and lush green vegetation, dotted with the lovely pale lavender of the early blossom of jacaranda trees. Here in the valley it is 7–8° hotter than Leopard Rock and more humid. Ideal for growing bananas.

The stiff green fronds of the banana trees stretch over 120–130 hectares, as far as the eye can see. At its most prolific, the plantation produces about 1,300,000 kilos of bananas. Blue polythene bags cover the unripe bunches of fruit, creating microclimates to speed ripening. The bags also prevent the bananas from being scratched and marked by their own leaves, causing imperfections which make them less attractive at market.

Everywhere there is activity. Tractors pull trailers of singing, chattering plantation workers, laughing children and women scurry around with enormous bunches of green bananas balanced on specially woven platforms on their heads. In the midst of the plantation is the farm. It has the charm of an old Devon holding,

46

except that the barns are constructed from bamboo and the stacked crates are full of bananas. Peacocks watch from the bonnets of Land Rovers.

A small track leads into the village, one of four that house the plantation workers and their families in the now-familiar thatched mud huts. The people here speak in the Shona dialect. Chickens with tiny fluffy yellow chicks peck around pots and pans set on open fires. Here, as throughout most of Africa, the staple diet is mealie meal (or mealie pap, as it is often called) and stew. Women are feeding their babies and the children play together with crude toys made from tin cans and wire. With the help of some of the men of the village, we dig out an underground fire.

There are many ways of cooking in the ground, all variations on a theme. In Thailand they roast chicken in a tin in a hole in the ground, covered with flaming straw. By the time the fire dies away the chicken is cooked to perfection. In rural France they pack hedgehog in clay and cook it in a similar fashion. When the clay is solid it is cracked off, pulling away the prickles.

In Victoria Falls Ray Stocker talked of a well-known guide who would catch a fish, gut it and wrap it in wet newspaper, then make a small fire in the ground, put the fish into the ashes and cover it with elephant dung. In the smouldering fire the fish smoked and cooked, and when the newspaper was pulled away the scales would come away too, leaving the succulent flesh. Tomorrow I intend to do something similar with fish, but today I am going to do something I have never done before: make a pudding in front of the cameras. What is more I shall attempt to bake it in an underground oven. The pudding is a banana custard and I have no idea whether it will work...

A pit has been dug and a fire lit on top of it. When it has burnt down to ashes these are shovelled inside the pit. Traditionally such ovens were used to cook madumbe, a black, sweet baking potato similar to a yam, while a stew cooked on the fire above. I whip up

What is this strange man doing..?

my custard, pour it over a layer of bananas in a ramekin dish and sprinkle it liberally with brown sugar. It is sealed inside the oven and the fire kept burning on a metal sheet on top, to provide all round heat.

While I wait and wonder what will happen to the pudding, I will cook a dish of rabbit with cream and bananas. As I wait for the crew to set up, I set an enamel teapot of water to boil on the fire so that we can make some coffee. Kim asks me what I am cooking next. 'Rabbit, old boy,' I say.

'What, in a teapot?'

A cry of amazement goes up from the villagers as I flame my dish of rabbit in brandy. They have never seen such a thing before. Twenty minutes later we remove the metal sheet from the top of the oven and peer inside. My pudding has puffed up like a soufflé and the custard has cooked perfectly. It tastes quite delicious. The villagers tuck in approvingly. Cooking with bananas is an entirely new idea for them.

Plantation Banana Custard

Serves 2

4 egg yolks	2 bananas, sliced
300ml (½ pint) double cream	soft brown sugar
drop of vanilla extract	

Beat the egg yolks, then blend in the cream. Add the vanilla extract. Lay the slices of banana in the bottom of a ramekin dish and pour the custard on top. Sprinkle with the sugar and bake in an under-ground oven or at 180°C/350°F, gas mark 4 for about 20 minutes.

ABOUT BANANAS

- The life cycle of a banana plant is between nine and fourteen months.
- Planting is staggered to produce fruit all year round, though the winter months, from May to July, are the most prolific.
- The bananas are picked at 70 per cent maturity, then artificially ripened for the local market or exported green to South Africa.
- The artificial ripening cycle takes five days, in which the temperature is gradually lowered from 18°C to the keeping temperature of 14°C. For the first day ethylene gas (which is produced naturally by bananas as they ripen) is introduced to speed up the process.

Rabbit with Bananas

Serves 4

3 Cox's apples, peeled, cored and
    sliced
25–50g (1–2oz) butter
1kg (2¼lb) rabbit, jointed
2 onions, finely diced
pinch of mustard
pinch of ground ginger
pinch of cinnamon
pinch of curry powder
good dash of brandy
300ml (½ pint) chicken stock

150ml (5fl oz) double cream
2 bananas
salt and freshly ground black
    pepper

For the Caramelized Apple Garnish
100g (4oz) white sugar
50ml (2fl oz) water
2 eating apples, skinned, cored
    and each cut into 8 slices

Put the sliced Cox's apples in a pan with 25g (1oz) of butter, cover and cook until the apples are soft. Reserve.

To make the caramelized apple garnish, put the sugar and water into a heavy-based saucepan and heat to dissolve the sugar. Bring to the boil, then continue to cook without stirring until the sugar caramelizes (be careful not to let it burn). Carefully add the apple slices and coat them in the caramel. Lift out with a couple of forks and cool on a wire tray.

Heat a little butter in a pan, put in the rabbit pieces and cook for 5 minutes, until brown. Lower the heat, add the onions and sweat for 2–3 minutes. Stir in the spices and cook for a few more minutes. Pour on the brandy and flame. When the flames die down, add the chicken stock and apple purée and simmer for 20–25 minutes until the rabbit is cooked and the sauce has reduced. Stir in the cream.

Slice the bananas and add to the pan. Heat through, then season to taste. Serve garnished with the caramelized apples.

DAY 10

MANYERA LAKE

Beyond the beautiful bamboo warehouses raised on stilts where tobacco is hung to dry, and past the silver and black wattle trees whose bark was once used for tanning leather, is the Manyera Lake. In the still of the early morning a pair of fish eagles call out to each other. Scott brews coffee and cooks breakfast on an open fire, while the rest of us dig out another underground oven. I push out into the lake in a dugout boat and cast my line. I am joined by Don Cripps, whose job is to look after transport and maintenance at Leopard Rock. He is an intelligent and informed man and an excellent fisherman. We talk a little about the country, about the transition from Rhodesia to the present Mugabe government and the new situation in South Africa.

We land some trout and an excellent bream. I wrap the trout in damp newspaper, moulding it like papier-mâché around the fish, and place it inside a tin in the underground oven. But the quality of the charcoal is poor and though the fish cooks to perfection inside the newspaper, it takes nearly six hours. In the meantime I build a little barbecue (or braai as they are called here), grill my bream and rustle up a delightful little spicy sauce.

We snake back up the mountain. Women sell embroidery on the roadside. They fix their samples of napkins and handkerchiefs to long sticks, like gaily decorated bunting, and wave them to attract the attention of motorists. In the clear afternoon light I see the Leopard Rock Hotel for the first time. It is an imposing muted pink building with thatched roof and turrets and a beautifully landscaped eighteen-hole golf-course. A bell-hop gloriously decked out in royal blue and gold steps forward to greet me.

RIGHT: Zimbabwean Bream, which I served with a little chilli, pineapple and ginger salsa

BELOW RIGHT: Preparing trout in newspaper for the underground oven

Zimbabwean Bream with Chilli, Pineapple and Ginger

Serves 2

1 whole bream

salt and freshly ground black
  pepper

squeeze of lemon, plus wedges of
  lemon for garnish

1 small bunch of coriander

vegetable oil

6 spring onions, cut lengthways

2 tomatoes, skinned, seeded and
  finely diced

½ large red chilli, cut into
  julienne strips

½ large green chilli, cut into
  julienne strips

25g (1oz) fresh root ginger, cut
  into julienne strips

2 rings fresh pineapple, cut into
  small dice

2 tablespoons dry sherry

1 tablespoon chopped chives,
  plus some for garnish

1 tablespoon soy sauce

Gut the fish (leave the scales on – they will stop the flesh from burning on the barbecue). Season the inside of the fish, add a squeeze of lemon juice and put in the coriander. Barbecue for about 4–8 minutes on each side, depending on the size of the fish.

Heat a little vegetable oil in a pan, put in the onions, and let them colour slightly before adding the tomatoes, then the chillies, ginger and pineapple. Stir-fry for a few moments, then pour in the sherry. Stir, taste and season if necessary. Add the chives and finally the soy sauce. Remove from the heat.

Lift the fish on to a serving dish, carefully peel away the skin from the top side, and sprinkle with a little soy sauce. Spoon over the sauce, and garnish with a few more chopped chives and lemon wedges.

DAY 11

HARARE TO JOHANNESBURG

At Harare airport Sheila and Scott are only just allowed out of the country due to irregularities incurred at the Zimbambwezi border. This is also becoming a recurring event. There is something funny about Sheila and Scott, I think. Sheila is accused of lying because she doesn't have one of the forms taken from her by the Zimbambwezian officials, and Scott has a wrong date stamped in his passport. Eventually the stony-faced officials relent. Tim is threatened with prosecution for standing on a chair. Every piece of the crew's equipment is examined by hand and Kim's bag full of film takes so long to search that he almost misses the plane to Johannesburg.

DAY 12

PARTY TIME IN JOHANNESBURG

Johannesburg is considered to be one of the most dangerous places in the world, but in the warm midday sunshine the city seems relaxed and free of the fear which stalks it at night, when men with guns walk the streets and no one leaves their car door unlocked for fear of being hijacked.

The Fishmonger is a bustling, merry little restaurant in one of the city's many shopping precincts. It has red-checked tablecloths and serves excellent shellfish and fish in little frying pans accompanied by fat chips or rice. At lunch with Sheila and Tim we become instantly entangled with a crazy bunch of people having a birthday party. They are mostly women with apparently huge appetites for life and strong opinions on everything. They have names like Polly Toothpick, Gillie Bean and Bart Tender. Much later I arrive back at my hotel just in time for a night out on the town with 'Marvellous' Mike Connor. And I can tell you he's quite a groovy dancer, but I won't mention it to his wife, as long as he doesn't lose his hat again. (He has fair, rather thinning hair and pale skin and suffers terribly from sunstroke. I've already bought him three hats and he's lost them all.) Anyway, I will simply say that it was a big night that left us with only ten minutes to pack for the red-eye flight to the island of Madagascar, some 250 miles off the east coast of Africa.

The plane from Harare to Antananarivo is crammed with athletes returning from the 6th All African Games, resplendent in green, white and red tracksuits, the colours of the national flag. Two of the girls have won gold medals at tennis. Within minutes of take-off they are singing and dancing in the aisles. It is a joyous flight. Even the little breakfast pots of preserves contain delicious real marmalade and jam. In order to make space for the athletes the crew has been asked to send all the equipment cargo, so there are no cameras to record the fun.

DAY 13

ANTANANARIVO, MADAGASCAR

There are places that tear the soul and churn the emotions. The former French colony of Madagascar is one of those places. It is pregnant with fear, excitement, danger and passion. It appals and yet it delights.

The road from the airport leads past paddy-fields into the outskirts of the capital, Antananarivo, known locally as Tana. The stench of exhaust fumes and burning rubber hangs over the pink brickwork houses and crude ironwork balconies. In contrast, the old town and administrative capital, with its skyline of palaces, is perched on the hill above, one of the Twelve Sacred Hills of Madagascar.

Officially there are eighteen different tribal groups. In reality there are many more. The influences are French, Creole, Indian, Arabic, Malaysian, Chinese and above all Indonesian. The majority of people are slight in the oriental way. The poorest people who scratch a living on the plain below the old town are of mainly African descent.

On the roadside women sell odd buttons from single trays, one offers an iron and a ball of recycled wool. Another peddles nuts and bolts and junk rescued from dustbins. There is no refrigeration and the meat that is for sale is black with flies. Ox-carts weave around delightful old flat-nosed Renault trucks, bull-nosed Peugeot cars and tarpaulin-covered pick-up trucks and in the market place children are playing football with a live rat.

My hotel, the Hilton, is run down and decorated in seventies fashion. It is populated by seedy businessmen who look like extras from *The French Connection*. The chef, Luke Bolleu, is a genuinely committed cook who cares very much about Malagasy food, and after a long cool local beer called Three Horses Brew and a few hours of chat I am fired by his enthusiasm.

DAY 14

THE ZOMA MARKET, ANTANANARIVO

They say that the Zoma market in Antananarivo on a Friday (Zoma actually means Friday) is one of the biggest outdoor markets in the world – then it would be, wouldn't it? Originally built in a grid-formation to house sixty to eighty steep-roofed stalls, it has grown far beyond its original conception and within the sprawling, babbling, trading place everything from furniture to food is for sale. Chickens cluck around bales of straw, and we buy some

They say the Zoma market is the biggest in the world

excellent cylindrical charcoal stoves, one made from a halved car wheel, one lined with terracotta. Elsewhere we find polished cast-aluminium casseroles and cauldrons. All perfect for cookery sketches in wild terrain.

Chillies, fresh ginger, spices and vanilla (the country's biggest export) are piled high, there is an aroma of fresh baguettes and there are casseroles bubbling over charcoal fires, filled with rice, shrimps, lamb and tomatoes, pork chops, white haricot beans and little beef patties. I have a plate of beef ribs, spinach and rice, which costs 2,000 francs (about 37 pence). It is delicious.

Shops in Antananarivo

For dessert there is kuba, a lovely rich and aromatic kind of cake made with rice flour, brown sugar and crushed-up peanuts, wrapped in banana leaves and poached in a bain-marie. In the market it is sold in slices.

Surrounded by truncheon-wielding security guards, we set up the first cooking sketch in the midst of the bedlam. Despite the happy faces and eagerness to please, poverty stalks all around, spawning a sub-culture of prostitutes, gangsters and thieves. It appears that the government is about to resign, there are no police working and the place is lawless and confused. Where once there was a little pickpocketing there is now armed robbery, kidnapping and hijacking. In the market place the thief who steals from his countrymen runs the risk of being lynched or beaten by an angry mob, but a tourist separated from a Rolex watch or Gucci handbag is unlikely to be given much quarter.

Many of the stallholders earn so little, they sleep under their stalls at the mercy of the rats, and although their tables are piled high with fabulous foods and the countryside is fertile, the vast majority of people are without the resources to buy them. Inflation has risen by about 50 per cent over the last eighteen months, and the average monthly wage, fixed by the government, is the equivalent of about £10 – only enough to buy rice for an average family of six for a fortnight. In one of the crazy legacies left by the French, foie gras (from duck, not goose) is cheaper than a bottle of Heinz tomato ketchup. The country's vast rich resources of gold, sapphires and quartz are sold abroad, as are lobster, prawns, and, of course, vanilla, but the money returns to the 200 or 300 families in whose hands the wealth of the island is concentrated.

While the crowd press round, laughing and waving, and children shout '*basa, basa*' (white man, white man), I cook three dishes simultaneously. The first is romazava, the national dish of beef, pork and chicken cooked with garlic, ginger, tomatoes and brèdes, a kind of spinach. Then there is the festival dish of pork

and eel stew, and a duck and ginger stew, in which the duck is initially cooked rather like a confit.

The Malagasy enjoy fatty, virtually unseasoned meat stews, but to cut through the fat they add a relish, rather like an Indian sambal, called sakay, which is a trilogy of minced ginger, garlic and red chilli. They also serve various salads as an accompaniment. The one that I prepare is called rougail, which is a salad of chopped red onion, spring onion and tomatoes, mixed together with a little salt.

We return to the hotel and, warned against the dangers of walking the streets after dark, I settle in for the night with a good simple meal of nasi goreng, served with little kebabs and an excellent refreshing salad of grated runner beans, cabbage, carrots and crushed peanuts, tossed with lime juice, garlic, oil and salt. This is a version of the raw vegetable salad (sometimes more like a pickle) known as achard, which was to recur throughout our travels in many forms and with many different spellings according to region and individual whim.

The hotel nightclub is populated by hookers and more jaded-looking businessmen. Apparently when the girls come in, the management take their identity cards. These are only returned when the guest who entertains them phones through to say that nothing has been stolen and their room is still intact.

Waiting, hoping, patiently...

Romazava

This is the national dish of Madagascar, made with beef, pork and chicken. The beef is added first, followed by the pork, and finally the chicken, the idea being that all the meats end up perfectly cooked at the same time. The flavourings of onion, ginger and garlic are added near the end of the cooking time to give a punchy, slightly crunchy kick to the rich sauce. You can use spinach instead of the local leaves (known as brèdes).

Serves 6

groundnut oil

450g (1lb) braising steak, cut into 5cm (2in) chunks

450g (1lb) leg or shoulder of pork, cut into 5cm (2in) chunks

450g (1lb) chicken, jointed

1kg (2¼lb) tomatoes, skinned and roughly chopped

2 onions, sliced

8–10 garlic cloves, crushed

50g (2oz) fresh root ginger, cut into julienne strips

450g (1lb) fresh brèdes or spinach, torn in pieces if the leaves are large, and washed thoroughly

salt and freshly ground black pepper

Heat a little oil in a large pan and briefly seal the beef, without browning. Add enough water to cover, bring to the boil, and simmer, covered, for about 30 minutes.

Add the pork and simmer for another 30 minutes or so, then add the chicken and simmer for about 10 minutes.

Add the tomatoes and continue cooking until they have melted around the meat to form a thick sauce. Add the onions, garlic and ginger and cook for about 10 minutes, until they have been absorbed into the tomatoes and meat juices, but are still quite al dente. At the last minute throw in the brèdes or spinach and stir until the leaves are just cooked through. Do not let them overcook.

Season to taste, and serve with Sakay and Rougail (see page 69).

Pork and Eel Stew

A festival dish, for happy occasions. Sakay, a mixture of ginger, garlic and chilli, is used as a condiment instead of salt and pepper. It is very hot and should be used sparingly. Rougail is a salad of red onions, spring onions and tomatoes that is served as a refreshing and contrasting accompaniment to the pork, which in Madagascar is always extremely fatty.

ABOVE: Cooking pork and eel
LEFT: Antananarivo market

Serves 6

groundnut oil

1.6kg (3½lb) leg or shoulder of pork, cut into 5cm (2in) chunks

700g (1½lb) eel, skinned and boned (ask your fishmonger to do this for you)

salt

1 large onion, sliced

700g (1½lb) tomatoes, skinned and roughly chopped

For the Sakay

75g (3oz) fresh root ginger, minced

8–10 garlic cloves, minced

15g (½oz) red chilli, minced

For the Rougail

1 red onion, chopped

6 spring onions, chopped

3 plum tomatoes, skinned and chopped

good pinch of salt

First make the Sakay and then the Rougail by mixing together the ingredients.

Lightly oil a large pan and seal the pork without colouring. Add enough water to cover, and simmer for 40 minutes to 1 hour, covered, until the meat is tender.

Cut the eel fillets into pieces about 10cm (4in) long and roll up. Sprinkle with salt. Add to the pan with the onion and tomatoes. Simmer for about 15 minutes until the eel is tender.

Serve with a little Sakay and Rougail.

Duck and Ginger Stew

At first sight this dish seems rather crude, but in fact it has interesting influences in the form of the confit of duck (or goose) so beloved of the southern French, and the Chinese twice-cooked duck.

Serves 4

4 duck joints (skin and fat left on)

2 red onions, sliced

25–50g (1–2oz) fresh root ginger, according to taste, cut into julienne strips

8–10 garlic cloves, crushed

1kg (2¼lb) tomatoes, skinned and roughly chopped

salt and freshly ground black pepper

Put the duck joints into a large pan and cover with water. Simmer, uncovered, for at least an hour until the water has evaporated and the duck is cooked and sitting in its own fat. Strain off the fat, then cover with a little more water, add the rest of the ingredients and simmer for about 25–30 minutes, until the onions, ginger, garlic and tomatoes coat the duck in a thick sort of marmalade.

Season to taste, and serve with Sakay and Rougail (see page 69).

DAY 15

MADAGASCAR PADDY-FIELDS

The paddy-fields are waiting for the rains, and in their semi-dry, semi-flooded state they have a bizarre beauty. Men and women are cutting out little seeding patches, the men digging and the women smoothing the earth over the seeds with a stick. In some places the little rice plants are already pushing through, creating brilliant green plots like billiard-tables dotted around the deep terracotta-coloured landscape. Later they will be transplanted in the crudely dug paddy-fields.

The banks of the canals which run through the area are strewn with drying laundry and in the dirty water and stagnant ponds men and children wade waist deep to spear fish. Elsewhere they have staked out small nets and traps. Some are trying to catch carp, lowering an old sheet into the mud and raising it, hoping that among the filth will be a fish. Eels, the local delicacy, are a good catch. The biggest eel I have ever seen dangles from a stick erected by a roadside vendor. It must weigh 8lb.

Everywhere there is filth and squalor, but it has a strange, compelling charm. Etched against the paddy-fields like Aztec stairways are piles of bricks, handmade from the clay which is dug out to create the ridges of the paddy-fields. The bricks are left to dry in the sun, then straw is burnt inside the brick stacks to fire the clay. Later the bricks will be used to build huts and houses.

Any day now the cyclones and tornadoes are expected. Each year they devastate the island, threatening these frail houses, causing massive floods and destroying roads, which outside of the capital are already rough and basic.

Rice paddy in the afternoon, Madagascar

A pretty girl has four carp to sell, which we buy, and in the lovely soft light of the late afternoon I cook a very happy dish of carp fillets with local green peppercorns and fresh vanilla. I have never cooked with fresh vanilla before. What a delight to scrape out the caviar-like seeds with their intense, sweet flavour. Behind me villagers from an island which can be approached only by a small canal punt backwards and forwards in dugout boats bearing rice, bicycles, children and prams.

Cooking carp

Carp with Vanilla

Vanilla sauces are terribly fashionable in London at the moment. In Madagascar they have been making them for ever. I had the luxury of making this with fresh vanilla and fresh peppercorns, but you will probably have to substitute dried ones. I also used mandarin eau-de-vie, a local speciality, which gives the creamy, slightly spicy sauce a lovely orangey flavour.

Serves 4

approx. 900g (2lb) carp (or perch, trout or bass)

salt

50g (2oz) butter

1 tablespoon green peppercorns

75ml (3fl oz) mandarin or orange eau-de-vie, or orange liqueur

250ml (9fl oz) fish stock

200ml (7fl oz) double cream

1 vanilla pod, split lengthways

For the Garnish

½ a lime or lemon

sprig of parsley

De-scale, clean and fillet the fish. (Ask your fishmonger to do this for you if you prefer.) Season with salt.

Heat a frying pan and put in half the butter. When it is hot add the fish, flesh side down, and fry for about a minute, until slightly coloured. Turn and cook for a further minute or so. Add the peppercorns and cook for a moment to bring out the flavour, then add the eau-de-vie and flambé. When the flames have died down remove the fillets and keep warm.

Add the fish stock to the pan and reduce until you have a syrup. Add the cream, and scrape the seeds from the vanilla pod into the sauce. Cook for about a minute. Cut the remaining butter into small pieces and whisk into the sauce.

Pour the sauce over the fish and garnish with the lime or lemon and parsley.

The stagecoach provides
popular and cheap transport ...

DAY 16

A VILLAGE OUTSIDE ANTANANARIVO

It is Famadihana, the day of the Turning of the Bones. In a country where life is cheap and death is easy, this ancient ritual of reburial encourages the idea that there is happiness after death.

The ceremony takes place once every few years all over Madagascar (or whenever the families can afford it). Everyone returns to the village of their ancestors to remove the dead from the tombs and wrap them in new shrouds, amid singing, dancing and great jollity. The tombs are a focal point of life here. The people already know which place has been allotted to them in their ancestral burial chamber, and death holds no fear.

The celebrations are held over two days. Last night a band played primitive New Orleans-style jazz, with violins, drums and bugles, and several hundred people joined in the singing and dancing. Today another band plays and the feast begins. Everyone turns out in their best colourful clothes, the women wearing pretty hats. The much-loved fatty beef stew is served from halved oil-drums. Rice is spooned from aluminium cauldrons two feet in diameter. People sell lollipops and ice-cream.

... because most of the cars don't go

In the baking heat and dust of midday, the happy party turns into a procession which winds its noisy way towards the tomb. The wrought-iron outer door is opened. Behind it another stone door is pulled back to reveal seventeen shrunken corpses laid on shelves. In a scene of great joy and celebration, the bodies are lifted out one by one and laid across the knees of the women who sit four abreast beside the tomb. New cotton shrouds are wound around the bodies, which are then wrapped in raffia. They are held aloft and taken around the tomb seven times before being reburied. The doors swing shut on the remembered dead. Outside, the living will continue to party for some time to come.

Dancing with the dead

DAY 17

A ROADSIDE IN MADAGASCAR

There are times when I have to remind myself that I am a cook and that my job is to prepare food for the television from whatever local ingredients I find around me. I am not a missionary or a social worker. But as we unload our new stove for a cooking sketch in the countryside, the entire crew and I are numbed by the poverty around us and nagged by the Madagascar paradox, that although the most exquisite foods are available here, it is beyond the means of the majority of the people to enjoy them. However, as I cook my dish of chicken and prawn curry, it is impossible not to be heartened by the joyfulness of the people who gather round to watch.

Chicken and Prawn Curry

Serves 4

2 teaspoons ground turmeric

5 tablespoons curry powder

4 garlic cloves, roughly chopped

25g (1oz) fresh root ginger, roughly chopped

salt

4 chicken breasts, halved diagonally

groundnut oil

2 onions, finely diced

1 teaspoon thyme

1 tablespoon chopped fresh parsley

5 tomatoes, skinned, seeded and very finely diced

300ml (½ pint) coconut milk

1 tablespoon chopped fresh coriander

24 large prawns (for example, tiger pawns), head on, tail removed and de-veined

juice of 1 lime

Koba is a delicious sweetmeat made from rice flour, crushed peanuts and brown sugar, which is then rolled in a banana leaf and poached in a bain-marie. It tastes a bit like marzipan

Mix together the turmeric and curry powder with just enough water to make a paste. Pound the garlic and ginger in a pestle and mortar.

Salt the chicken. Heat a little oil in a large frying pan and fry the chicken until golden, then add the onions, garlic and ginger and sweat until soft. Add the turmeric and curry powder paste and cook for 2–3 minutes. Add the thyme, parsley and tomatoes and cook for 10–15 minutes. Stir in the coconut milk and heat through. Add the coriander, remove from the heat and reserve.

In a separate pan, heat some more oil and pan-fry the prawns for a minute or so. Add the lime juice and season with salt.

Place some chicken in the centre of each plate, spoon the sauce around it, and arrange the prawns on top of the sauce.

DAY 18

THE MICHELIN TRAIN

'Micheline'

Criss-crossing Madagascar is a magnificent infrastructure of railways and associated buildings: storehouses, stationmasters' offices, platforms and stations. But like so much on this entrancing island, the network has fallen into appalling disarray. Abandoned goods vans have been commandeered by the homeless, and the graveyards of rusting locomotives and rolling stock would have the eccentric beauty of crazy sculpture if it weren't for the terrible poverty they symbolize.

But amid the neglect we find a genuine piece of early twentieth-century folly, apparently one of only two of its type left in the world, known as the Michelin train. In fact, it is not really a train, but a rail-car, built in thirties style, with a long bonnet and inflatable tyres. The idea was originally patented in 1859 by a Scotsman and immediately derided as totally impracticable. But around 1930, the tyre manufacturer André Michelin, after a sleepless night aboard a train listening to the clacking of the wheels as they trundled over points, ordered his son to find the patent on the inflatable-tyred train and develop the notion. The result is an amazing piece of Art Deco engineering which seats about forty or fifty people on wicker chairs, next to a small bar.

The train trundles off around the island, but TV cheats that we are, we plan to fake a breakdown as an excuse to get out and cook against the spectacular patchwork of dark red hills and valleys and vivid green plots of rice seedlings. In fact, in Mike's attempts to have the train stop on a sixpence, it breaks down quite naturally.

While it is being mended I make an electrifyingly hot soup of chicken and ginger and an elegant dish with smoked duck, mango and fresh pink peppercorns. To keep Chris happy I also prepare two vegetarian dishes: a spicy achard of vegetables and a rice dish made

with chillies, ginger, tomatoes, peppers and brèdes. Unfortunately, when he disappears scrambling up the railway bank to set up a wide shot, I absentmindedly combine the chicken and ginger soup with the rice to make a lunch dish for our guests on the train. By the time Chris returns there is only the achard to satisfy his vegetarian appetite.

ABOVE: Waiting for a train

RIGHT: Making a quick snack while the 'train' is being repaired

Smoked Duck Breasts with Mango and Pink Peppercorns

Of course, what made this simple dish special was the fresh pink peppercorns which, along with the green ones, are easily available in Madagascar.

Serves 2

2 smoked duck breasts, sliced thinly lengthways

2 mangoes, peeled, halved and thinly sliced

1 head frisée lettuce, picked and washed

For the Dressing
1 teaspoon pink peppercorns

6 tablespoons groundnut oil

good squeeze of lime juice

1 tablespoon chopped fresh coriander

1 teaspoon finely chopped fresh root ginger

2 garlic cloves, finely chopped

6 thin segments of lime

salt

Mix together all the ingredients for the dressing.

Arrange the duck and mango around the edge of two plates, pile the frisée in the centre, and drizzle everything with the dressing.

Chicken and Ginger Soup

Adjust the amount of ginger according to your taste – personally I like plenty of it.

Serves 4–6

1.5 litres (2½ pints) chicken stock (or use chicken carcass and water, etc.)

1 onion, studded with 4 or 5 cloves

salt and freshly ground black pepper

700g (1½lb) chicken, skinned, boned and diced

1 onion, finely chopped

75g (3oz) long-grain white rice

25–50g (1–2oz) fresh root ginger, cut into julienne strips

juice of at least 3 lemons (according to taste)

salt

1 bunch of coriander, roughly chopped

Simmer the stock or the chicken carcass or bones with the clove-studded onion and some salt and pepper for approximately 25 minutes.

Strain the stock into a clean pan and add the chicken pieces, chopped onion and rice. Simmer until the chicken is cooked and the rice is tender – about 15–20 minutes (don't let it overcook). Add the ginger and lemon juice.

Season to taste, then serve, garnished with plenty of chopped coriander.

Achard de Legumes

This chopped vegetable salad is found all over Madagascar. It is served on its own, as an hors d'œuvre, or as an accompaniment to stews, designed to cut through the fatty food the Malagasy love. At the markets, stall-holders chop the ingredients with a mandoline, and it can be bought ready-made. Malagasy mustard seeds are tiny, rather like poppy seeds, so do not need to be crushed. The ones you buy in Britain do.

Serves 6–8

½ a white cabbage, shredded

6 carrots, grated

3 onions, halved and finely sliced

100g (4oz) French or runner beans, sliced

handful of fresh peanuts, crushed

salt

For the Dressing

2 very small red chillies, chopped

25g (1oz) fresh root ginger, chopped

3 garlic cloves, crushed

100ml (4fl oz) groundnut oil

40ml (1½fl oz) white wine vinegar

1 teaspoon curry powder

1 teaspoon mustard seeds, crushed

½ teaspoon ground turmeric

First mix together all the ingredients for the dressing. Toss the vegetables in the dressing, sprinkle with the peanuts and season with salt to taste.

LEFT: Chicken – a rare treat –
most people eat rice and greens

Savoury Stir-fried Rice

Serves 2

groundnut oil

2 red chillies, chopped

50g (2oz) fresh root ginger, cut into julienne strips

1 onion, finely chopped

3 garlic cloves, finely sliced

2 green peppers, seeded and cut into julienne strips

225g (8oz) long-grain rice, cooked

5 tomatoes, skinned, seeded and finely diced

large handful of brèdes or spinach, torn in pieces if the leaves are large, and washed thoroughly

salt and freshly ground black pepper

1 tablespoon chopped fresh coriander

Heat a little oil in a wok. Add the chillies, ginger, onion, garlic and green peppers and stir-fry for a few minutes. Add the rice and tomato dice. Stir-fry for another minute or so. Toss in the brèdes or spinach and season to taste. Stir-fry for 2–3 minutes, then sprinkle on the chopped coriander and serve.

DAY 19

MAJUNGA

The flight from Antananarivo to Majunga on the northern coast of Madagascar in two noisy light planes (a Piper Chieftain and a Cessna 402), takes about an hour and forty minutes, after a comic scene in which every piece of the crew's gear is weighed on a set of bathroom scales.

A fine palm-tree-lined promenade sweeps majestically across the bay from the port of Majunga. There is an ornamental garden, called Le Jardin des Amours, but it is derelict and unkempt. In the port ancient and distressed wooden twin-masted boats rest in the mud of the low tide, and trampships lie rotting. In the distance sail-driven trading vessels trundle up and down the coast transporting charcoal and raffia.

In another life this must have been a stylish holiday resort, built on a grid system with wide boulevards and elegant buildings with wrought-iron New Orleans style balconies and fine filigree doors. A grotesque concrete cathedral is strangely out of place amid the decadent romance of the place, there are potholes in the roads and many of the houses are boarded up and crumbling, while people live in shacks behind.

As dusk falls women set up braais on the beach and whole families gather round to eat small satay-sized brochettes of zebu (horned cattle). Majunga, with its large port, is at the centre of the seafood and fishing industry, but none of the fish is for sale to the local people, except at high prices in restaurants.

The outrageous beauty, so typical of Madagascar

Majunga – north-west Madagascar

DAY 20

MAJUNGA

We have arrived with some trepidation because Majunga is in the grip of the plague. There have been twenty-one reported deaths. The disease is carried by rats such as the one that scuttles frequently between the kitchen and the courtyard of the crew's hotel, which looks like an abandoned set from the film *Casablanca*.

My hotel seems to be populated by charming rogues. It is run by a former French military man who is doing his best to present the kind of bistro you might find in the 16th Arrondissement in Paris. Surrounded by intriguing local produce, he complains that he can't find crème fraîche or Roquefort.

The local speciality is flavoured rum, however, and, as we discovered last night, the hotel makes an excellent version. Orange, lemon and lime peel is cooked down in a pan with vanilla pods, passion fruit and mango to form a thick syrup. This is put through a fine sieve, then mixed with the rum, together with some fresh vanilla pods and ginger. Then it is left to mature. The result is lethal but fabulous. But I reckon you don't need to go to all that trouble – just some sliced ginger added to a bottle of rum would be terrific.

By 10 a.m. it is already so hot that nothing is moving – except the rats. It might be the aftermath of the rum or just my romantic soul, but I feel sure that everyone here is a gunrunner, diamond smuggler or mercenary. I see people who look desperate and washed up, yet they are still determined to enjoy themselves in this town which is so much more laid back, in its faded decadent way, than Antananarivo.

Before I actually begin to believe that I am the Rick character in *Casablanca*, and that Ingrid Bergman is about to walk through the door, I give myself a shake. There is filming to be done.

Going fishing... sailing on this boat was exhilarating and so fast

We join some fishermen on board one of a small fleet of pirogues, dugout sailboats about twenty feet long with a single short mast and two outriggers, which fly across the water with an astonishing and exhilarating turn of speed. With prawns as bait we drop hand-lines in a bid to hook some tuna, but we catch nothing. The crew transfer to the motor support boat to film on the way back to port, but the propshaft has sheered off and it has to be towed back by our speedy sailboat.

DAY 21

OFF THE MAJUNGA COAST

The coastal trading vessel is a twin-masted spritsail cutter that transports raffia. Raffia work, in which the strands are split into about eight strips and woven and knotted into delicate rugs and mats, is a thriving cottage industry on this part of the island. The boat has a wonderful wobbly gangplank and every joint on board is covered in tar. By the time we have finished filming, there is tar over most of the flight cases, and for some reason, over most of Steve.

I prepare to cook on a charcoal stove in a wooden bunker on deck, while Mike tries to redirect the natural movements of sun and wind to suit the camera. By the time everyone is happy the wind drops and the sail slumps almost over my table as we begin the sketch. Nevertheless it is good fun, and my dishes of fish stew and marinated red mullet are warmly received by the boat's crew, although there are some complaints that I haven't put enough marijuana in the food. In fact, I don't have any marijuana, but apparently these fellows use it a lot in their cooking.

As we reach the shore, in the full heat of the afternoon, I make the mistake of walking barefoot over the scalding sand, almost blistering my feet. We are to cook at the home of Andrew and Michael, friends of our local fixer Simon and his charming girlfriend Ange. On their verandah I prepare a stir-fry of prawns with mango and ginger.

Cooking on board

Fish Stew – Aboard a Sailing Trade Schooner

The only fish I could find on the Sunday morning before we sailed was crayfish and bream – you can use any fish and shellfish you like.

Serves 4 or so

groundnut oil

335g (12oz) potatoes, diced

1 large carrot, diced

1 onion, diced

1 leek, roughly chopped

4 garlic cloves, finely chopped

1 red chilli, chopped

25g (1oz) fresh root ginger, cut
  into julienne strips

salt

1 x 2kg (4½lb) crayfish or lobster,
  flesh cut into about 8 pieces

1 black bream, approx. 1.6kg
  (3½lb), filleted

150ml (5fl oz) fresh coconut milk
  (or tinned coconut milk
  diluted with water)

juice of 3 lemons

chopped fresh coriander

For the Tomato Sauce

75ml (3fl oz) olive oil

10 tomatoes, roughly chopped

salt and pepper

First make the tomato sauce. Heat the olive oil and add the tomatoes. Cook gently for about 20 minutes until you have a thick sauce. Season, reserve and keep warm.

Heat a little groundnut oil in a large pan. Add the potatoes, carrot, onion and leek, cover the pan, and cook for 5–10 minutes. Add the garlic, chilli and ginger and cook for about 5 minutes. Now add the tomato sauce and mix well.

Salt the fish lightly and place it on top of the vegetables. Add the coconut milk and lemon juice, pop on the lid and cook until the fish is ready (just a few minutes). Garnish with chopped coriander.

Malagasy Marinated Fish

Red mullet is ideal for this.

Serves 4

4 x 175g (6oz) red mullet, filleted

1 red chilli, very finely chopped

15g (½oz) fresh root ginger, very finely chopped

2 garlic cloves, very finely chopped

10 spring onions, finely chopped

100ml (4fl oz) mixed lemon and lime juice

100ml (4fl oz) olive oil

100ml (4fl oz) coconut milk

salt

Place the mullet on a non-metallic plate. Combine all the other ingredients, sprinkle liberally with salt, and put into the fridge for 2–3 hours until the fish has 'cooked' in the marinade.

Lacking in confidence

Prawn, Mango and Ginger Stir-fry

I made this with the local prawns known as Camerons, which are about 15cm (6in) long – about six or seven to the kilo – and the excellent local unrefined rum.

Serves 2–4

groundnut oil

4 carrots, cut into matchsticks

small bunch of spring onions, cut lengthways

2 green chillies, seeded and roughly chopped

2 red chillies, seeded and roughly chopped

40g (1½oz) fresh root ginger, cut into julienne strips

3 garlic cloves, finely sliced

10 plum tomatoes, skinned, seeded and diced

salt

12 large prawns, the biggest you can find, heads taken off and shelled except for the tail, de-veined and butterflied (that is, cut lengthways along the back)

2 mangoes, skinned and cut into wedges

4 tablespoons rum

Heat a little oil in a wok. Add the carrots and stir-fry for 30 seconds, then add the spring onions and stir-fry for a minute. Add the chillies, half the ginger and the garlic and stir-fry for 30 seconds. Add the tomato dice and stir-fry for another minute. Season. Remove and place in a warm serving dish.

Wipe out the pan, add a little more oil, and when it is very hot quickly seal the prawns on both sides (they will open out like butterflies). Add the remaining ginger and the mangoes. Splash in the rum and flambé.

Arrange the prawns, ginger and mangoes with their pan juices on the bed of stir-fried vegetables.

DAY 22

THE BLUES

Lunch at my hotel turns into a party by the pool. Someone picks up a guitar and as the sun beats down we sing the blues and misbehave appallingly – not a story for this book, I'm afraid. Wait for the autobiography!

DAY 23

TO JOHANNESBURG

Scott and Adrian are almost arrested (this is getting to be a habit) when Scott attempts to take a photograph of the President's Palace in Antananarivo's Upper Town. His film is ripped from his camera and his instinctive angry reaction nearly lands him in the interrogation room. At the airport I am asked by a man dressed as a gendarme to buy a bottle of duty-free whisky and give it to him before I board the plane. I leave Madagascar in a turmoil of mixed emotions.

Steve has been in touch with an official at Johannesburg airport, who remembers seeing his distinctive missing box of equipment. Unfortunately it was heading for London at the time. He has arranged for it to be collected at Johannesburg when we arrive. But when our flight lands the official is off duty and no one knows anything about the box.

DAY 23

EASTERN TRANSVAAL

SEAGOON: 'I want you to accompany me on the safari.'
BLOODNOK: 'Gad, sir, I'm sorry, I've played one.'
Spike Milligan, *The Goon Show*

When Theodore Roosevelt went on safari in Africa in 1909, the presidential caravan stretched out over a mile, with up to 500 porters bearing hundreds of animal traps, 4 tons of salt for curing skins, scales for weighing game, about sixty tents including a skinning tent and mess tent, tons of Boston baked beans, and the President's personal selection of books, specially bound to endure the expedition.

The Floyd crew arrives with forty-three pieces of assorted baggage and flight cases of equipment, a few pots and pans and a charcoal stove bought in Madagascar. In my briefcase I have a Mars bar and several paperbacks.

We reach the Londolozi Game Reserve alongside the Kruger National Park in the Eastern Transvaal after a six-hour drive from Johannesburg on a wide modern road that cuts first through the flat scrubby countryside of the Highveld then through the Drakensberg Mountains, 2,250 metres above sea level. As night closes in thunder crashes behind the hills. Forest fires blaze intermittently beside the road as we enter the Lowveld, known as the food basket of Southern Africa, with its huge banana plantation, its profusion of fruit and vegetables, sugar and macadamia and pecan nuts.

Here and there are shanty towns, littered with beaten-up rusty old cars. A massive factory lit up like a fairground belches out foul fumes. It is a paper and pulp manufacturer, one of several in the region.

The last part of the journey is over a rough track through the darkness of the bush. Lanterns held aloft like beacons and the sound of welcoming voices usher us in to Londolozi Lodge bush camp. A slender, attractive blonde lady called Robyn holds out her hand. In the dim light I make out a notice. It says that lion, leopard, rhino, elephant and buffalo are to be found in the Reserve, and that there is no physical impediment to them entering the residential area. It says that the Reserve accepts no responsibility whatsoever for injury, death, loss or damage, and that all guests enter and use the facilities offered entirely at their own risk. Under no circumstances is a guest to walk in the camp at night unless accompanied by a guard.

By lantern light we are escorted to a cheerful verandah overlooking the bush. In the vast darkness hyenas shriek and big cats prowl. They are at their most dangerous under cover of the night. But inside the lodge with its profusion of African fabrics, pottery and wonderful wirework bowls and trays, the sofas are big and welcoming and jugs of Pimms and fresh fruit cocktails wait on a long table. As we sip our drinks, Robyn cheerfully hands around indemnity forms for us to sign. They reiterate the fact that the camp will take no responsibility if we are eaten by wild animals. Still, the atmosphere is jolly and our beaming waiters, Welding and July, are swift to replenish glasses. Refreshed, we are escorted by lamplight to rooms in thatched bungalows, known as rondavels. We pretend not to listen for sounds in the bushes or jump at unexpected shadows. A guard will fetch us in half an hour for dinner.

Lamplit dinner in the boma, a kind of pit fenced off from the bush by a bamboo fence, is a festive, tasty affair of kudu kebabs and lamb cooked on the braai, served with vegetables and a delicious selection of relishes and chutneys. We retire early amid the calls of the creatures of the night.

ABOVE: Most reassuring...

LEFT: Africa sunset

DAY 24

LONDOLOZI GAME RESERVE, BUSH CAMP

In 1926 at a Johannesburg tennis party, Charles Boyd Varty bought a piece of land in the Eastern Transvaal for the equivalent of about 2s 6d a hectare. He had never even seen the territory. But the old railway line to Mozambique ran through it and he and his party hunted on the land, travelling part of the way by train, the rest on horseback, or with oxen and bearers.

Nearly fifty years later in the darkest days of apartheid Charles Boyd Varty's grandsons John and David had a dream: to conserve this same land for Africa's wildlife and to create an integrated community of black and white South Africans working together and sharing in the success of the venture. So Londolozi was created, followed by the Conservation Corporation with its ever-expanding number of luxury lodges. The brothers' avowed intent is to conserve ever more land in order to turn South Africa into a safari paradise. And the men and women who work for them have an almost missionary zeal and dedication to promoting the 'ConsCorp Ethic'.

In the village above the lodge there is a crèche, a school, a soccer pitch, a shop in which everyone has a share, and a restaurant, serving bottled beer and various combinations of porridge, meat, chicken and rice. Many of the huts are encircled with painted bands like ribbons, which depict the householders' trade. Moses the handyman has painted saws, hammers, bicycles, screwdrivers and paintbrushes. The potmaker has pictures of urns. There is a shoemaker, a tinsmith, someone who sews, a carpet maker and small paper recycling industry which produces notepaper for the lodges.

The ever-smiling, wise-cracking Welding, who says that his role in life is to bring people together, tells us how Africans traditionally have a tribal name, but also a more light-hearted name given by the family, often relating to something that happened or was seen on the day of birth. So many of the staff have names like Promise and Excellent. In the kitchen there is a cook called Lettuce, and the security man is called Stolen.

Dinner is once again a jolly affair in the dimly lit boma. At dawn we will go out in search of the Big Five: lion, leopard, rhino, elephant and buffalo.

Ingredients for impala and fruit curry

DAY 25

LONDOLOZI GAME RESERVE

As the sun rises we head into the bush. Gradually our eyes adjust to the shapes, colours and shadows and we begin to spot movement: first impala, then wildebeest. John, the Ranger, signals for quiet. Ahead is a pride of fourteen lions, resting sleepily in the shade after a night of hunting. They pay little attention to the familiar quiet purr of our special, game-viewing Land Rover or the sight of Chris's camera. A pregnant leopard stretched out in the grass, panting as the heat rises, is equally uncaring and two elephants having a mudbath are quite oblivious of our presence, but graceful giraffe tread closer, peering inquisitively.

The walkie-talkie crackles into action. The rest of the team are gathered on a stretch of bank beside the River Sand, which runs through the reserve. Over the radio I hear hippos laughing and belching. They are waiting for me to cook.

I build my fire in a wheelbarrow and set a wok over the coals. Backed up by the hippo chorus, I make an impala curry with coconut and some of the wonderful dried fruit of the area. I serve it with samp, which is a coarse version of mealie meal.

Impala Curry

This is the one I cooked on my wok over a wheelbarrow full of charcoal, beside a river full of hippos. And, by the way, impala tastes rather like venison.

Serves 4

vegetable oil
1 onion, chopped
900g (2lb) fillet of impala or
    venison
2 garlic cloves, chopped
2 red chillies, chopped
1 teaspoon ground fenugreek
1 teaspoon ground chilli
1 teaspoon ground cumin

1 tablespoon tomato purée
large handful of dried fruit
    (include apples, bananas,
    apricots, pears, prunes, figs,
    etc.)
400ml (14fl oz) coconut milk
bunch of fresh coriander,
    chopped

Heat a little oil in a wok or large pan, add the onion and sauté until slightly coloured. Add the impala or venison and brown. Add the garlic, chillies and spices and stir thoroughly, then add the tomato purée and dried fruit. Cook for a few minutes, then pour in the coconut milk. Simmer until the meat is tender (about 20-30 minutes). Sprinkle with coriander.

ABOUT HIPPOS

- Hippos kill more people than crocodiles, because they overturn boats and can trample people on land.
- They can weigh up to 2 tonnes.
- They eat about 130kg of grass a day.
- At night when they come out of the water they often walk up to three kilometres in search of grass.

DAY 26

THE BIG BREAKFAST

Nature's great master-piece, an Elephant,
the only harmless great thing, the giant of beasts.
John Donne

Outside the camp the crew are loading equipment into safari vehicles for the morning's shoot. I am about to climb into the Range Rover. From the bushes behind comes a crunching noise. We turn and come face to face with an elephant. A film crew has never scattered so quickly.

Heading up the path Scott, Sheila and Adrian stop dead in their tracks. Our ranger, Justin, motions them to back up slowly and quietly to the safety of the camp. They must clamber over a wall and scramble down a bank before creeping up to the vehicles from another direction. As they jump in and we take off I christen the elephant Hector.

On a rocky ledge in the bush I join some of the cooks from Londolozi and the nearby Singita Lodge to prepare breakfast. With them is Yvonne, the jolly, funny, former catering manager from Johannesburg who has transformed the kitchens at Londolozi, and Mark, the ranger from Singita whose quick wit and irreverent sense of fun stands out amid the almost evangelical fervour of many of the staff.

Dumi, whose last name, Ndlovo, means elephant, is simmering warthog sausages in champagne before barbecuing them on a braai. Beside him blonde Ashleigh is cooking an accompaniment of green mealie griddle cakes made from fresh corn pounded until it is creamy, mixed with flour and eggs. She will top the cakes with apple slices caramelized with brown sugar, cinnamon and butter.

Sina and Rachel grill kebabs and cook a huge flat omelette with mushrooms and bacon, while Deirdre from Singita rustles up an enormous kedgeree. My contribution to the feast is a big pot of porridge, cooked over an open fire and made with whisky and pistachio-flavoured honey and enriched with double cream. It is, pronounces Mike, absolutely marvellous.

Too close for comfort

Behind us, right on cue, Hector the elephant ambles into shot, chomping on branches as he approaches. We finish cooking and as Hector vanishes into the distance his brother Oliver makes his entrance. As we clamber a little way down the rocks to get a closer shot of him he turns and, flapping his vast ears and bellowing, he charges. In a flurry of stones and dust we hurtle back up the rocks. 'Only a mock charge,' says ranger Mark. 'Just a warning.' Of course. Anyway, he couldn't have made it up over the rocks. 'Oh, yes he could,' says Mark, grinning. 'If he had really felt like it.'

This evening, due to pressure of space at Londolozi, we are to transfer to a private lodge called Castleton. At first, as our small convoy pulls up at a lonely group of low buildings, my heart sinks. The bush stretches as far as the eye can see, the landscape broken only by a waterhole a few hundred yards from the lodge. But inside a large comfortable room a polished wood dining-table is surrounded by tall chairs, there are sideboards filled with books, well-chosen china and bottles of wine, whisky and gin. Sofas cluster around a huge fireplace, there are rugs on the floor, and hunting trophies decorate the walls beneath a slow-turning fan. On the verandah are more sofas and wicker chairs with huge cushions, and, to the delight of the crew, a pool table. Across the yard is a kitchen, with prettily painted cupboards and checked curtains, and the bedrooms in individual thatched bungalows are decorated cosily.

As the night closes in a wind whips up and a storm threatens. We eat a simple, pleasing dinner by lamplight, crack open a whisky bottle and play pool and tell stories until the early hours. Like servicemen thrown together on a dangerous mission in some remote and unfamiliar place, we find a special kind of camaraderie.

Hanging around watching the
world go by

DAY **27**

CASTLETON LODGE

In the morning giraffe, zebra, kudu and wildebeest take turns at the waterhole and baboons prance and jump through the trees, while local ladies like culinary sisters of mercy, in starched white aprons and head-scarves, serve breakfast. Today is a day off and later I will cook for the crew. I spend the rest of the morning in the quaint kitchen with Scott preparing crispy deep-fried onions, vegetable curry, salads and sambals. We fire up my trusty wok in the midday sun and I make a kind of chicken biryani-cum-paella in which Africa meets India and Spain with a twist of Floyd.

Lunch is taken at a table laid on the grass, and then we gather inside to watch the semi-finals of the rugby union Currie Cup, played out among South Africa's top provincial teams. The match is between Natal and Free State. If Natal win, the final will be held in Durban next weekend and we will be there.

Natal do win.

ABOUT GIRAFFES

- The name giraffe comes from the Arabic xirapha, which means one who walks quickly.
- Seventy per cent are killed by lion, hyena, etc. before they reach maturity. Once pulled down, there is no hope for them.
- They have seven vertebrae, just like other mammals, but to prevent a sudden rush of blood to the brain when they spread their legs and bend down to drink, they have an intricate circulatory system which relieves the pressure.
- The male grows to around 5.5 metres (the female is about a metre shorter).
- Their main food source is the foliage of the acacia tree.

YVONNE'S TALE

Yvonne Short is in charge of the kitchens at Londolozi Game Reserve.

'I came here with my husband from Johannesburg eight years ago when John and David Varty decided that if they were going to make a go of safaris, they would have to be the very best – and that included the food. At that time cooking here meant boiling a piece of topside or mutton until it was blue and making a flour and water sauce to go with it.

'The Vartys also wanted to involve the local community. They have always been progressive, quite controversial, forward-thinking. The ending of apartheid wasn't an issue here, because we have always been integrated.

'We started from scratch in the kitchen. I had been in catering management and didn't know much about cooking, but I knew how to get things together and make things happen. We built up a collection of books and food magazines and taught the chefs – and ourselves – as we went along. We said to the waiters and the scullery people and the gardeners: 'What do you like doing?' 'What do you want to do?' Some of them said they'd like to be cooks, so we said: 'OK, come into the kitchen'.

'Since not many of the people could read and they spoke only Shangaan (an off-shoot of Shona), we made recipes with pictures cut from labels on tins and packets. If we couldn't find pictures of ingredients we drew them. Eventually we developed our own kind of shorthand, and gradually we taught everyone to read the recipe books. It's been very exciting, we have some great cooks and we're all very proud of our kitchen.

'South African cuisine is only just finding its identity. We have fabulous ingredients here but they haven't always been used in a very interesting way. People say they want to taste African food, but that is mealie and stew, and you soon get tired of it. So we are developing what we call Cross-cultural Cuisine, in which we are using traditional ingredients like maize and beans and samp and maroj (a kind of wild spinach) in a stylish way.

'Everyone works eight weeks on and two weeks off, and they can choose to live nearby or have a room at the staff village. Most of the men who work here have more than one wife. They have an official one at home, and when they come to work here they take other wives and have more children. One of the staff here has about thirty-four children in all. Since the man is only obliged to look after his official family, and his wages often go home to them, the unofficial family often has little financial support. So we have a school and a crèche and a clinic here, so that the extended families are looked after, and many of the women are involved in making crafts which are supplied to the camps, so they can earn money.

'The idea is that everyone should benefit from the reserve being here. Everyone is taught that nothing is a hassle. It is a challenge. We are excited about life. That is the ethic.'

The following recipes were given to me by Yvonne at the Londolozi Game Reserve.

Nut Oil

mixed whole nuts,   groundnut oil
  roasted
fresh herbs

Place the roasted nuts and herbs in a sterilized bottle. Pour the oil over the top and leave to stand for at least 3 weeks for the flavour to develop.

Citrus Oil

unwaxed lemon peel,   lemon thyme
  pith removed   groundnut oil
unwaxed orange peel,
  pith removed

Place the peel in a sterilized bottle with the lemon thyme. Pour in the oil and leave to stand for at least 3 weeks for the flavour to develop.

Whole Garlic and Chillies in Oil

whole garlic bulbs,   fresh coriander
  roasted   groundnut oil
whole chillies, red and
  green

Roast the garlic bulbs in a hot oven, 200°C/400°F/gas mark 6, for 15–20 minutes. Allow to cool. In a sterilized jar, layer the whole roasted garlic and whole chillies, sprinkling with coriander as you go. Pour in the oil and seal the jar.

Roasted Pepper Preserve

mixed red, green and   whole garlic cloves
  yellow peppers,   fresh herbs
  halved and seeded   groundnut oil

Put the peppers on a baking sheet, skin side uppermost, and roast them in a hot oven to blister the skins. Peel the peppers and place the flesh in a sterilized jar, with the whole garlic cloves and fresh herbs. Cover with oil and store in the fridge for up to 8 weeks.

Preserved Lemons

whole unwaxed lemons   fresh thyme
rock salt   lemon juice

Cut the lemons into quarters, not quite through. Layer with rock salt and fresh thyme in a sterilized jar. Heat the lemon juice in a pan and pour over enough to cover the lemons. Seal the jar. Leave for at least a month for the full flavour to develop.

Homemade Chilli Paste

whole red and green   white wine vinegar
  chillies   sunflower oil

Place the chillies in a heavy-based saucepan. Cover completely with vinegar and finish with a layer of oil. Simmer for at least 3 hours, until the chillies are soft. Blend in a food processor. Put into small sterilized jars, refrigerate, and use within 1 month.

Lemon and Olive Preserve

lemons, sliced thinly   fresh thyme
black olives   groundnut oil

Layer the lemon slices, olives and thyme in a jar that will seal. Cover with oil and leave in the fridge for at least 1 month for the flavour to develop.

Green Mango Atchar

Makes about 4 litres (7 pints)

3kg (6½lb) green   1 litre (2¼ pints)
  (underripe)   vinegar
  mangoes, peeled and   1 teaspoon ground
  roughly cubed   ginger
250g (8oz) seedless   ½ teaspoon salt
  raisins   1 teaspoon chilli
400g (14oz) caster   powder (optional)
  sugar

Place all the ingredients in a saucepan, bring to the boil, and simmer until the chutney thickens. While still hot, seal in a sterilized bottle.

DAY 28

FULL STEAM AHEAD

A Cessna Grand Caravan aircraft waits at the landing strip. As we drive the few miles from the lodge at Castleton we come across a lion and lioness breathless from mating. Under a tree close by a second male crouches panting. We pull up within feet of him. He is a gloriously handsome creature with the icy stare of the assassin. A magnificent killing machine only a spring away.

We linger silently for what feels like an age while Chris films and Mike hopes for an MGM roar for the title sequence of the programme. Still the lion crouches and watches, and with secret relief we move on towards the runway.

The flight is silky smooth and four minutes later the Cessna touches down at Skukuza airport in the Kruger Park. We transfer to a bus for the drive to the border town of Komatipoort which serves as the customs point between Mozambique and South Africa, and where the Rovos Rail steam train 'Pride of Africa' waits to transport us to Pretoria.

Giraffes run alongside the bus and occasionally we must stop while they cross the road. We pass herds of wildebeest, rhino, buffalo and impala roaming through the bush close to the road, and, hours too early, arrive at Komatipoort. The porters have not yet come on duty, but the 'Pride of Africa' waits majestically in the station, and in the sweltering midday sun we load trolleys with our forty-three pieces of luggage and equipment and climb aboard.

RIGHT: The waterhole

Rovos Rail was conceived when Rohan Vos, a man who made his money in the motor industry and invested it in property, decided in 1989 to buy a few carriages and a locomotive as a kind of family hobby; a 'caravan' on the tracks. The railway authorities weren't terribly happy about the idea, but told him he could run his train if he sold tickets. So six and a half years later the 'Pride of Africa', with its lovingly restored carriages, dining car and observation car (the lounge bar) mostly dating from the twenties and thirties, runs between Pretoria and the Kruger Park, Cape Town and Victoria Falls. There is also a twelve-day journey from Cape Town to Dar es Salaam, which takes in game drives, the Victoria Falls and a sunset cruise on the Zambezi.

As the journey begins through the Transvaal, once populated by gold prospectors, I take my shift in the galley kitchen, preparing a classic steak chasseur. With ostrich steaks. After dinner we repair to the comfort of the observation car, with its wooden bar, easy chairs and scattered novels and picture books telling of great train journeys.

There is a romance about steam trains. And there is an excitement about sipping cocktails in a lounge car, dressed in a dinner jacket, watching the track reach vanishing point, which can go to a man's head. I say this because at two in the morning, playing Humphrey Bogart for the sixth take of the ultimate cocktail-mixing scene, it finally occurred to me that it might be more sensible if everyone went to bed.

DAY 29

ABOARD THE 'PRIDE OF AFRICA'

I have cooked on every conceivable kind of boat, on ox-carts and desert islands, on the manifold of a jeep and even on the back of an elephant. I have prepared banquets for the finest chefs in France and cooked for the Vietnamese army, but this morning we filmed the best cooking sketch of my life. There are small boys and grown men everywhere who would give their eye-teeth to do what I did this morning: I fried bacon and eggs on a spade in the hot box of the engine of a steam train. I think I'll become a train spotter next.

At midday we pull into Pretoria, the administrative capital of South Africa. The pavements of the city are carpeted in purple blossom which has fallen from the jacaranda trees. Now in full bloom, they line the city's avenues and in the warm swirling wind their flowers fall like confetti.

Inside the bar of the 100-year-old Victoria Hotel, close by Pretoria station, the inevitable slow fan turns, there are prints and paintings of steam trains on the walls of the gently faded, comfortable bar, and palms in enormous tubs are dotted around the gracious twenties-style dining-room.

After a happy lunch of some excellent fish we drive to the secluded Mount Grace Hotel, about an hour's drive from Pretoria. Tomorrow we will leave for Johannesburg airport to take the flight to Durban. According to the guide-books the city is famous for its Golden Mile of beaches, its surfers and – since the city houses the biggest Asian population in South Africa – its curries.

DAY 30

A ZULU WELCOME

Through the window of the South African Airlines flight from Johannesburg to Durban I see an extraordinary crowd gathered on the tarmac. We are in the third largest city in South Africa, in KwaZulu Natal province, home to the Zulu heartland. There are women in tribal dress and a troupe of Zulu dancers doing their stuff in boiler-suits and wellington boots alongside a bunch of chefs in sparkling whites. As we make our way to the terminal building the entire crew is showered with beaded necklaces and garlands made from flowers and bananas. I am ceremoniously presented with a Zulu spear and swamped by photographers and journalists. After weeks of relative anonymity in Zimbambwezi, Madagascar and the Eastern Transvaal, the return to the world of media attention comes as a shock.

We are joined by Ezra Singapi, who will be our mediator and fixer for the remainder of our trip. He is a sharply intelligent, politically aware man who treats some of our more crazy requirements with an easy sense of humour. It was a pleasure to have him along. As we drive to the Royal Hotel near the city hall the sky above the city suddenly erupts with the boom of engines and trails of red, white and blue smoke. The Red Arrows are also in town.

DAY 31

DURBAN

*A single girl should never accept food from an unmarried man;
there may be a love potion in it.*
(*Old Shona taboo*)

The rain is lashing down in Durban. The famed golden sands look grey and sad and the surfers have stayed away. Today my picture is in the papers. I am a 'food fundi' (someone says this means expert).

This morning, in the harbour, in a blustery scene on board a tug called the *Bart Grove*, beneath a sign which read 'in case of fire close vents', I cooked lamb curry on my charcoal stove and served it with assorted sambals and pickles to Captain Dave Filmer.

But right now I am surrounded by women. About twenty of them and counting, tucking into crayfish and mussels and heaps of seafood tagliatelle in a restaurant somewhere on an Avenue named Florida. Every time I look up there seem to be more women arriving.

Last night in my excitement at seeing a big city again, and on a whirlwind tour of the nightspots, I apparently invited half the female population of Durban to lunch. And they called up their friends and invited them, too. Still, worse things happen at sea…

Tugboat Curry (Durban)

This is based on a recipe given to me by the Royal Hotel. They make their own curry powder, which consists of approximately 4 tablespoons chilli powder to 1 tablespoon ground turmeric and ½ tablespoon each of ground cumin, cinnamon and cardamom (since this recipe also uses a cinnamon stick, you could leave out the cinnamon). The thick, rich sauce is created by long, slow cooking. Only add stock or water if absolutely necessary.

Serves 4

vegetable oil

2kg (4½lb) lamb leg, boned and
  cut into chunks

3–4 tablespoons curry powder, to
  taste

1 onion, chopped

1 cinnamon stick

1 good teaspoon chopped fresh
  root ginger

5 garlic cloves, crushed

8 tomatoes, diced

4 large potatoes, cut into large
  dice

a few curry leaves (optional)

bunch of fresh coriander

Heat a little oil in a large pan and add the lamb a handful at a time. Cook until browned and sealed. Add the curry powder and fry for about 1 minute. Add the onion, stir to coat with the curry powder, then add the cinnamon, ginger and garlic and stir again.

Put in the tomatoes and cook for 20–25 minutes, adding a little water if the mixture becomes too dry. Add the potatoes and continue to cook until they are tender – about 20 minutes.

Add the curry leaves and stir through, sprinkle with coriander and serve with Sambal (see page 168) and Lime Pickle (see page 132).

Lime Pickle

Every Indian cook has his or her own recipe for lime pickle. This is the method according to Luke Nair, Executive Chef of the Royal Hotel, Durban.

3kg (6¾lb) limes
600ml (1 pint) vegetable oil
50ml (2fl oz) lime or lemon juice
large pinch of salt
200g (7oz) masala pickle (an

equal mix of ground
cardamom, ground coriander,
ground chilli, mustard seeds
and ground turmeric)

Quarter the limes, and either dry in the sun for a few days or in a very cool oven for about an hour. Heat the oil, lime or lemon juice and salt in a large pan, add the spices and warm through. Put the limes into a large sterilized jar, pour the oil mixture over the top and seal. Allow the flavours to develop for a few days before using.

RIGHT: Durban? Houston? Or Birmingham?

FAR RIGHT: Cockling on a Durban beach

LEFT: With the boys at the Royal Hotel

DAY 32

GREY STREET, DURBAN

At 6 a.m. the upstairs kitchen of Patel's Vegetarian Refreshment Room on Grey Street is filled with the aroma of spices and the sound of oil sizzling. Barefooted staff scoop freshly made curry into enormous trays which are whisked downstairs to the café and shop. In the heart of Durban's Indian community, this is the home of bunny chow, the famous Durban meal of curry served in a hollowed-out loaf of bread. Behind the counter in the café, loaves with their centres already loosened are stacked like bricks. A steady stream of customers orders fillings of one or all of the four vegetable curries (made with combinations of beans, lentils and vegetables), and the centres of the loaves are popped on top like little hats. They will be used like scoops to eat the curry.

Elsewhere in the city bunny chow is made with lamb curry, but the original Gujarati meal is strictly vegetarian. Like the Cornish pasty or the Mediterranean pain bagna (hollowed-out bread filled with tuna, salad and olives), it is the worker's traditional all-in-one meal.

In the heat of the kitchen other snacks are being prepared. Great tin tubs are filled with flour and water paste flavoured with cumin. It is pushed through flat metal sieves to make a sort of spaghetti and deep-fried, then sold in bags. It is known as sev. Some of the sev is mixed with the thicker, more stick-like ganthia, together with fried peas and fried peanuts to make a kind of Bombay mix. Potato bhajiya are also being prepared: slices of potatoes dipped in a similar lightly spiced batter and deep-fried.

RIGHT: Indian nibblets

DAY 33

THE CURRIE CUP

The British are passionate about rugby. New Zealanders are passionate about rugby. *I* am passionate about rugby. But the South Africans are completely potty about it. Today the whole nation, but particularly the supporters of Natal and Western Province, are gripped by Currie Cup fever.

Ever the unbiased observer, I am standing in the pouring rain, my boots sinking into the mud outside the Kings Park Stadium, Durban, kitted out in a black and white Natal rugby jersey and hat. Bantering with the hordes of fans who press around me, I cook boerewors and steaks on a braai. Everywhere there are barbecues, stacks of meat and crates of beer. Raucous pre-match get-togethers are in full swing; those not lucky enough to have tickets will continue to party during the match, and after the final whistle the eating, drinking and celebrating will go on well into the night.

Inside the stadium the atmosphere is electrifying. I am overwhelmed by a roar of welcome, much back-slapping and sharing of hot toddies. Minutes later, amid great pomp and circumstance and a flurry of helicopters and flags, the match gets under way.

Even on a rain-sodden, muddy pitch the élite of South Africa's players brilliantly demonstrate the supremacy of Southern Hemisphere rugby. It is a match of international quality that has me gasping and leaves the outcome of the impending England v South Africa game at Twickenham in no doubt (rugby fans will now know that England were humiliated once again).

Everyone in Durban seems to be happy tonight. What is more, it is Stan's birthday. Back in the bar of the Royal Hotel we embarrass him with a cake, champagne and a chorus of 'Happy Birthday' to make the most vocal Natal supporter proud.

DAY 34

VICTORIA STREET, DURBAN

LEFT: The braai before the match

In the Victoria Street fish and meat market in the heart of the Indian sector of the city, stalls are laden with sheep's heads, tripe, tongue and every manner of offal, most of which will be curried in the homes of the local community. Fish stalls are impressively stacked with barracuda, salmon, salted snoek and rock cod. Many of these will also be used in curries – traditionally fish is curried in a sauce made with the juice of the tamarind.

Many years ago, here in Victoria Street, Chandrika Harie's great-grandfather started a tiny grocer's shop known as Haribhai's. Now the family business has grown into South Africa's biggest spice emporium, and changes in the law have meant that Indian traders may now buy premises outside the sector. So the company has moved to Pine Street, near the beach front.

In the warehouse, sacks are filled with gloriously coloured spices, and in the shop next door the shelves are packed with produce not only from India but from China, Indonesia, Thailand and Mexico. Upstairs Chandrika, a keen cook, and her husband, Vinod, are creating a kitchen area for demonstrations and workshops where local and visiting cooks of every nationality can produce vegetarian food. Chandrika says that they began stocking many of the ingredients in the shop when a stream of customers suddenly began asking for things like lemon grass, galangal and coconut milk. It seems that they had been watching a TV programme called *Far Flung Floyd*.

Curried Fish in Banana Leaf or Foil

This fish curry recipe was given to me by Chandrika Harie, whose family own Haribhai's Spice Emporium on Durban's Pine Street (even though she only cooks vegetarian food herself); it comes from *Indian Delights* by Zuleikha Mayat. It uses the pulp of the tamarind, which is traditional in fish curries in Durban. Tamarind fruit look like beans and when ripe their green flesh turns chocolate-brown. They have a sour taste with just a hint of sweetness. Usually the tamarind flesh is sold packed into blocks. This needs to be soaked in water and the pulp pushed through a sieve – but follow the instructions given. Or use lemon juice instead.

Serves 2–4

2 teaspoons coriander seeds

2 teaspoons cumin seeds

1 tablespoon chopped fresh
  coconut

½ teaspoon ground turmeric

2 teaspoons red or green chillies,
  seeded and finely chopped

1 teaspoon salt

1 medium onion, grated

2 teaspoons garlic cloves, crushed

small bunch of fresh coriander,
  chopped

1 tablespoon tamarind or lemon
  juice

1 tablespoon vegetable oil

approx. 1kg (2¼lb) whole fresh
  line fish (you could use a fish
  such as red mullet or salmon
  trout), gutted and washed

Grind the coriander and cumin seeds and pound with the coconut in a pestle and mortar. Add the rest of the spices and the grated onion, garlic and coriander and mix well. Add the tamarind or lemon juice and the oil and bind into a paste. Make a series of deep incisions along the top of the fish. Smear the fish inside and out with the paste and leave to marinate for a few hours. Preheat the oven to 200°C/400°F, gas mark 6. If using banana leaves grease them and then use to wrap the fish. Put on a tray and bake for 1 hour. If using foil, grease an ovenproof dish and lay the fish on top. Pour 2 tablespoons of vegetable oil over the top, cover with foil and bake for 40 minutes. Remove the foil and let the fish brown.

DAY 35

THE ROYAL HOTEL, DURBAN

There is a field several hours' drive north of Durban known as Rorke's Drift, where in 1879, during the Anglo-Zulu war, in the makeshift military hospital of a small British fort, around 100 soldiers held off 4,000 Zulus until a relief column arrived. They made the story into a film, *Zulu*, which inspired me to join the British army. My first post in Germany in the early sixties enabled me to travel freely throughout what we used to call the Continent, and as a consequence I discovered food. So I quit the army to become a cook. If I hadn't been a cook I wouldn't have appeared on television. And if I hadn't appeared on television I wouldn't have come to Africa. Which is why, from the moment *Floyd on Africa* became a serious proposition, in spite of the obvious attractions of hippos and elephants, mud huts and canoes, this was the one location I insisted we couldn't miss.

But each day, since the cruel elements closed in, the trip has been abandoned. Even I can see little currency in a cooking sketch filmed in fog somewhere in Africa. And now time has run out.

To make matters more painful, today I have been deep-fried by the press. The adulation has gone sour, and I am accused of refusing to cook for the King of the Zulus. So now the headlines say: 'No feast fit for a king' which I find rather sad, because without a fascination for the Zulus… but I have been through that. And they did omit to mention that a representative of the King requested a fee of several thousands of rands for his appearance.

No matter. Tomorrow we fly to Port Elizabeth, then travel by road to Plettenberg Bay in Cape Province, home of the Western Province rugby team. My Natal rugby jersey has been consigned to the bottom of my trunk.

THE ZULU'S TALE

Petros is a porter at the Royal Hotel, Durban. His family still live in a traditional Zulu village.

'When I am in Durban I live as everyone here does, but when I go to my parents' village I live as they do. They have a traditional thatched house, and the main food is mealie meal and beans. When I was little the beans would just be cooked with salt, but now they are often curried or cooked with spices. Sometimes we might have cabbage or sweet potatoes or yams, and sometimes my family will kill a fowl. If there is a party they might kill a cow.

'My father has two wives and six children in each family. All of us share the same house. The Zulu house has about ten rooms built in a circle with a living-room in the centre. One part of our house is for each mother, with the room in the centre for all of us.

'Next year I will probably be married, to a girl I have been with since 1987. In the Zulu culture we believe that you must be with someone you love for at least five years before you marry. But I think I will have two wives, like my father. We believe that if you only have one wife, she is not going to look after the home properly, because she is alone, with no one watching her, whereas my mother looks at the other mother and doesn't want my father to think that her side of the house is nicer. So they are in competition. It is the same with money. The one wife does not want her husband to think the other wife is more careful with the money he gives her.'

DAY 36

PLETTENBERG BAY

The resort of Plettenberg consists of a spectacular bay with wonderful creamy breakers smashing on to it and a modern strip of a town built around it. They say that when the weather is fine it is quite beautiful. Sadly it is cold and dull and Plettenberg appears to be shut.

Squid fishing is good fun though. I take my new gas-fired wok-machine (another good thing to come out of Plettenberg) on board one of

RIGHT: Hand-lining for squid

the modern, twin-hulled sixty-foot snub-nosed boats from which a crew of ten or twelve men fish for squid on hand-lines. These boats sit out in the bay for four or five days at a time, and to stave off the boredom the fishermen treat themselves to lots of ice-cream (the local code-word for ganja). I cook a dish of stir-fried squid with chillies and peppers and garlic. Unfortunately I also set fire to the boat. However, we manage to put it out and all is forgiven.

In a fit of mischief tonight I decide to unpack my Natal jersey and wear it to the local bar. I am nearly lynched.

Stir-fried Squid

Serves 4

3–4 tablespoons olive oil

450g (1lb) fresh squid, sliced into rings

2 onions, finely chopped

1 red pepper, cut into julienne strips

1 green pepper, cut into julienne strips

4 garlic cloves, finely sliced

3 dried red chillies, chopped

5 tomatoes, skinned, seeded and diced

good handful of spinach leaves, chard or similar greens

salt and freshly ground black pepper

4 tablespoons soy sauce

Heat the oil in a wok until very hot. Add the squid and onions and stir-fry for about 30 seconds. Add the peppers and stir-fry for a further minute. Add the garlic, chillies and tomatoes and cook for another minute or so. At the last minute stir in the leaves. Season, then sprinkle with soy sauce, toss and serve.

DAY 38

OUDTSHOORN

The *Floyd on…* programmes have always had an element of, not to put too fine a point on it, silliness, and today has been designated an extremely silly day. By now Marvellous Mike has lost another two hats, Rapid Kim has shot over 3,000 photographs and is missing, presumed eaten by an alligator. Miraculously he shows up in time for the drive to the town of Oudtshoorn in the region called Little Karoo, about two and a half hours from Plettenberg. It is a place known principally for ostriches. In the late nineteenth century, when ostrich feathers were essential fashion items for women, the local 'feather barons' built great palaces with their profits. These days the feathers are mostly used for dusters and the ostentatious palaces have largely fallen into decay. However, there is still a trade in ostrich skin (for bags and shoes), ostrich meat – either fresh or dried to make biltong – and the massive ostrich eggs which are sold in every tourist outlet in South Africa. Oudtshoorn has become a tourist destination for those who want to look at – or ride on – the world's biggest bird.

Nearby, for some reason, there is also a cheetah ranch, where someone has suggested I might do a cooking sketch. But at the cheetah ranch we have a small crisis. The press are waiting and a big sign says 'Welcome Keith Floyd'. Then I see the cheetahs in a little garden, rolling on their backs, sticking their legs in the air and purring. I make my excuses and leave, which, of course, provokes another virulent attack on me by the press, but I'm not interested in filming in zoos. The whole point of the programme we are trying to make is about freedom, freedom to cook, freedom to travel, and the freedom of animals to roam. Having said that, there is a case for arguing that too many South Africans and tourists know more about an elephant, its habits and habitat, than they do of the lifestyle of some 28 million 'invisible' people.

ABOUT OSTRICHES

- An adult ostrich is about 2.5 metres (8 feet) high and can weigh up to 150kg or so.
- The male plumage is black, with white wing and tail feathers. The females are grey.
- During the mating season the skin of the male turns bright pink and he roars like a lion if disturbed.
- An ostrich can travel at up to 50km (30 miles) per hour.
- An ostrich egg is equivalent to about twenty-four hen's eggs.

But I digress. At the Highgate ostrich farm about ten kilometres from town, coachloads of people are arriving. The birds are quite foolish creatures but highly amusing, and at least they are doing what ostriches do naturally. I tuck an ostrich feather in my hat and we unload the stove and set up a table in a field. About 100 ostriches gather around in a circle and watch. They don't seem to mind that I am preparing an ostrich stew.

Only when I have finished cooking do they suddenly charge at the table, greedily pecking at everything from the napkins to the salt pot, lifting the lid from the casserole and even trying to eat the hot charcoal. Chaos erupts and we beat a hasty retreat. By the way, ostriches don't bury their heads in the sand, and I have it on their authority that they never will.

Ostrich Stew

Ostrich meat is dark red and tastes rather like fillet steak. It is available in some specialist shops and supermarkets – but to satisfy my editor, I shall allow you to substitute fillet steak.

Serves 4–6

vegetable oil

2 onions, finely chopped

4 garlic cloves, chopped

1kg (2¼lb) ostrich meat, cut into chunks

5 large carrots, cut into chunks

100g (4oz) bacon, chopped

¾ bottle of red wine

1 tablespoon tomato purée

good splash of schnapps

2 bay leaves

1 large boerewors (available from delicatessens)

100g (4oz) mushrooms, quartered

Heat some oil in a large pan and add the onions and garlic. Cook gently for a few minutes until the onions are slightly softened. Add the ostrich meat and brown. Add the carrots, bacon, wine, tomato purée, schnapps and bay leaves and simmer for about 10 minutes. Add the boerewors and mushrooms and simmer for a further 20 minutes.

DAY 39

INTO THE HILLS

I have been told of a charming small town called Prince Albert on the edge of the Karoo, at the foot of the Swartberg Pass. I feel sure that there must be some little cheesemakers or sausagemakers there, or among the mountain farms and villages, where we might do a cooking sketch. While the crew film whatever general views they can, given the miserable weather, I set off with Stan for an adventure. We have a tin of sweets and drinks in the cool-box and the open road ahead.

To begin with it is a perfectly good road, but as we snake up the mountain we pass a sign that says 'Unsuitable for heavy vehicles and caravans', and the journey becomes terrifying. Heroically we press on to the summit, where, if one dared to look, there are apparently terrific views over the Karoo. The journey down to Prince Albert is even worse. Stan cheerfully points the Range Rover down the most precipitous, narrow, nerve-racking pass I have ever been over in my life. I have brought the Hi-8 video camera with me, to record anything interesting for Mike, but I can't even look out of the window.

Somehow we make it to Prince Albert, a sweet one-street town with single-storey Victorian and Cape Dutch houses, with slightly rounded roofs and little verandahs. There are neat gardens, miniature canals, a white painted corrugated iron church with a spire, and a tiny hotel in the middle.

We take the long route home. In my terror I forgot to look for any cheesemakers or sausagemakers in the area.

DAY 40

BOSSIESGIF TOWNSHIP

Beyond the luxurious holiday homes of Plettenberg Bay is the Bossiesgif township, with its collection of shacks erected from wood, corrugated metal and cardboard. Women wash clothes in the open air in bowls and tin baths, using water collected from standpipes. Close by stands a field. There is nothing in it but toilets. The authorities would like to move the township here, so that they can extend the industrial zone which separates the wooden shacks from the smart resort. They would like the people to build their houses around the toilets. But the people do not want to move.

Many of those who live here work in the hotels and restaurants in town. But over 50 per cent are unemployed. A kitchen nearby serves bean stew to those who have no work. Many of the tiny houses are home to extended families of cousins and aunts and uncles. As is traditional in African homes, the family, particularly children and elders, is all-important. Everyone is treated as a brother or sister and is welcome to share in whatever food and shelter can be provided.

We have been invited to cook inside the spartan but immaculate home of Onica Damane. She is a teacher and her sister Eunice does perming – which I now discover to be the local word for hairdressing. They are a jolly family and we have a happy time together cooking my version of a traditional chicken stew with mealie.

This evening in the bar I regale a load of new chums about my experiences in the township. Someone says: 'Only troublemakers go to townships.' We had no trouble. We had fun. I go over to the juke box and to my delight Bob Dylan's 'Blowing in the Wind' is E27. I press it and ask the barman to turn it up to the maximum. 'How many years can some people exist, before they are allowed to be free ..?'

LEFT: What was written on the door was true

151

Chicken Stew with Mealie

Serves 4

vegetable oil

1 large chicken, jointed, or
 several drumsticks

4 onions, quartered

4 garlic cloves, peeled

4 potatoes, skin left on, cut into
 chunks

5 carrots, cut into chunks

2 bay leaves

2 teaspoons black peppercorns

1 litre (1¾pints) light beer

1 large bunch of fresh parsley,
 chopped

salt

5 baby squash, halved

100g (4oz) mushrooms, halved

175g (6oz) French beans, halved

cayenne pepper

For the Mealie

175–225g (6–8oz) spinach

2 tablespoons vegetable oil

Aromat seasoning

salt

cayenne pepper, to taste

175g (6oz) mealie meal (maize
 flour, available from health
 food stores)

Heat some oil in a pan and fry the chicken, turning frequently, for 20–25 minutes. When almost cooked, remove from the pan and reserve. Put the onions and garlic into the pan and cook gently for a few minutes. Return the chicken to the pan, add the potatoes, carrots and bay leaves, peppercorns, beer and half the parsley, season with salt, then simmer for 20 minutes. Add the squash, mushrooms and French beans and cook for a further 10 minutes.

Meanwhile, make the mealie. Put the spinach in a pan with 300ml (½pint) of water and simmer for a few minutes until cooked. Add the oil, Aromat, salt and cayenne pepper. Allow to cool slightly, then add the mealie and stir well to stop it going lumpy. Cover and cook over a low heat for about 3 minutes. Stir well, cover again and cook for a further 5 minutes.

Sprinkle the rest of the parsley over the chicken and dust with cayenne pepper. Serve with the mealie.

DAY 41

CAPE TOWN

The journey from Plettenberg to Cape Town is uneventful and the weather still misty and unpredictable. My hotel, the Cellars Country House, is in the lush green suburb of Constantia, with its forest areas, botanical gardens and secluded houses with swimming-pools and immaculate lawns. It is also the home of South Africa's oldest wine estate, Groot Constantia. At one time its dessert wine was world-famous, and its grapes were once trodden by slaves. The winery with its early Cape Dutch gabled architecture still continues, though it is owned by the government and it is its near neighbour, Klein Constantia, whose sweet wine is attracting attention.

The elegant white buildings of the Cellars are surrounded by gardens filled with white roses. We are welcomed warmly and enjoy a good lunch of chicken biryani, piled into a filo pastry basket and served with sambals. As a fan of dessert wines I am eager to taste the much talked-about Klein Constantia Vin de Constance. It is delicious, though quite light, with a lemony, honey flavour.

Since the Cellars is full, the crew are being put up at a charming little guesthouse in Constantia, run by Lavinia and Terry Crawford-Browne. Lavinia is executive secretary to Desmond Tutu, and she and her husband are an enlightened, intelligent couple deeply committed to the New South Africa. When Nelson Mandela was finally released from prison on a Sunday afternoon it was decided that he must eat his first meal as a free man at Bishop's Court. Being Sunday, however, all the supermarkets were closed, so Lavinia had the job of rushing around Cape Town's small shops finding chicken for the celebration meal.

Groot Constantia Vinery

In the evening we wander down to the seafront. A strong south-easterly wind is buffeting the waves. It is known as the Cape Doctor, because it is said to blow away dust and pollution, purifying the atmosphere. Behind is Table Mountain and on a clear day Robben Island, the prison which held Nelson Mandela, is visible across Table Bay. This evening it is hidden in the mist.

The Victoria and Alfred Waterfront is the up-market face of the docks, an enormous complex of shopping malls, bars and restaurants, selling everything from tacos to fish and chips. But on the wrong side of the tracks, in the heart of the working port, is a long low wooden building with blue and white awnings called Panama Jack's. Inside, crayfish caught off the south-east coast at Port Elizabeth swim about in a seawater tank that is also filled with oysters. In the big open kitchen, cooks C.J. and Owen, who look like rock singers, cook fish and shellfish on an open griddle. There will be sardines, prawns, squid, and whatever is fresh that day: Cape salmon, musselcracker, dorado, marlin, swordfish, yellowtail, tuna…

It is a fun place that is quickly packed out with customers. We order mixed platters of fish and seafood which are served in big black pans, and decide to film here tomorrow.

LEFT: Swinging gospel singers from the Cape Town township

BELOW LEFT: Cape Town Harbour

157

DAY 42

PANAMA JACK'S

This morning, in a hectic, bustling cooking sketch with the kitchen of Panama Jack's in full swing around me, I make two hearty dishes which seem fitting in this inclement weather: a crayfish bisque and a mussel chowder. As we depart, the dishes are being added to the lunch menu with the note: 'As cooked by Keith Floyd'.

Crayfish Bisque

Please remember, as I said earlier in the book, that all cooking times and measurements should be taken with a large pinch of salt! The food is only cooked when you are happy with it and not because the recipe says so.

Serves 8

250ml (9fl oz) vegetable oil

3kg (6½lb) chopped live crayfish (include the shells and heads)

butter

4 carrots, diced

2 sticks of celery, chopped

3 onions, diced

2 leeks, chopped

1 garlic bulb, chopped

250ml (9fl oz) brandy

1 bottle of white wine

275g (10oz) tomato purée

15 very ripe plum tomatoes, halved

2 bay leaves

4 sprigs of fresh thyme

4 litres (7 pints) fish or chicken stock

a little mashed potato to thicken (if necessary)

salt and freshly ground black pepper

Heat the oil in a large pan until it is smoking. Add the chopped crayfish and cook hard until they take colour. Turn down the heat, add a little butter and put in the carrots, celery, onions, leeks and garlic. Sweat for 2 minutes or so.

Pour on the brandy and flame. Add the wine and reduce by half. Add the tomato purée and cook until the sauce thickens. Add the fresh tomatoes, herbs and stock. Cover and cook gently for ³/₄–1 hour. If necessary thicken with a little mashed potato. Put through a fine sieve, check the seasoning and serve.

Mussel Chowder

Serves 4

3kg (6½lb) mussels

1 teaspoon black peppercorns

2 bay leaves

6 stalks of fresh parsley (chop the leaves for the garnish)

4 sprigs of fresh thyme

1 bottle of dry white wine

butter

4 garlic cloves, chopped

3 onions, finely chopped

2 leeks, diced

4 carrots, finely diced

6 potatoes, diced

½ litre (16fl oz) double cream

1 teaspoon ground turmeric (or some saffron if you can afford it)

Wash the mussels thoroughly in plenty of swirling water, removing beards and barnacles. Discard any that are open. Heat a large pan and add the mussels, peppercorns, bay leaves, parsley stalks, thyme and about a third of the wine. Cover and cook until the mussels have opened. Discard any which do not open. Pour the contents of the pan through a conical sieve and reserve the juices. Leave about 16 of the mussels in their shells, and of the remainder leave half whole and chop the rest.

In a clean pan heat a little butter and sweat the garlic, onions, leeks and carrots. Add the rest of the wine and the stock from the mussels. Add water to cover if necessary. Bring to the boil, add the potatoes and cook until they are tender. Add the whole and chopped mussels and most of the cream and heat through. Add the turmeric or saffron, then drop in the mussels in their shells. Heat through once again, then serve with chopped parsley and a swirl of the remaining cream.

TABLE MOUNTAIN

Table Mountain is draped in a tablecloth of cloud. Legend says it is the smoke curling from the pipe of an old burgher – some say it is St Peter – trying to outsmoke the devil. And there are other superstitions. We have brought some crayfish 1,086 metres up by cable-car to the summit, but when the African conductor who has kindly carried the container of lobster looks inside he runs away in a panic, shouting about 'water spiders' and evil spirits. Apparently the African people are frightened of crayfish, crabs, spiders and snakes.

Here I think we should pause for a quick geological lesson so I can explain that Table Mountain is not, in fact, a single mountain, but the northernmost bit of the Cape Peninsula mountain chain, to which it is joined by a promontory called Devil's Peak. The summit is also populated by little creatures called rock dassie (or hyrax), which, although they are diminutive furry things, are the closest living relatives of elephants, in that their front teeth are really tiny tusks and they have three toes.

But back to the cooking. I grill my crayfish, and as the sun bursts through the clouds I serve it up with a piri piri sauce and lemon and fines herbes butter to two climbers called Gillian McKirdy and Trevor Mackenzie who with perfect timing happen to pop over the summit, in the wonderful way of television.

Table Mountain

Table Mountain Crayfish with Piri Piri Sauce and Lemon and Fines Herbes Butter

Serves 2

2 crayfish or lobster

salt

2 tablespoons vegetable oil plus a little extra for brushing the crayfish or lobster

2 garlic cloves, finely chopped

½ a red pepper, finely diced

½ a green pepper, finely diced

½ a yellow pepper, finely diced

100ml (4fl oz) piri piri oil (available from specialist grocers and delicatessens)

chilli powder, to taste

For the Lemon Butter

100g (4oz) butter

juice of 2 lemons

1 tablespoon fresh mixed herbs (parsley, chervil, tarragon, chives, basil and dill)

salt and freshly ground white pepper

Halve the crayfish or lobster, season with salt and brush with oil. Place on the barbecue, shell side down first so that when the oil flames the shell burns, rather than the flesh, cook for a few minutes until half done, then turn it over and finish cooking.

Heat 2 tablespoons of oil in a wok or large pan, add the garlic and peppers and stir-fry for a minute or so. Add the piri piri oil and chilli powder. Season with salt and cook for about 30 seconds, then pour into a bowl and reserve.

Melt the butter in a pan, add the lemon juice and bring to the boil. Add the herbs and season. Serve the crayfish or lobster accompanied by the piri piri sauce and the lemon and herb butter.

DAY 44

THE WATERFRONT

Cape Town seems to be made up of lots of microclimates. On one day in different areas it can be starkly sunny, blustery, cloudy or raining. In Constantia it is sunny, but on the waterfront the Cape Doctor is again blowing ferociously.

I am making a bredie, a dish made famous by the Cape Malays, the descendants of the Muslim Indonesian and Malay slaves who were brought to South Africa by the Dutch in the eighteenth century. In 1830 they were freed, and many settled in the area of the city called Bo-Kaap, with its winding streets and early eighteenth-century cottages. Many of the slaves were highly skilled artisans, and they have made their mark not only in the culinary tradition of the Cape, but also in the city's architecture.

The rich Malay cuisine is invariably spiced and curried and often uses quite sweet sauces. Typical are soesaties (marinated pork and lamb grilled on skewers and served with rice and cooked fruit) and bobotie, a baked dish of minced meat with herbs and spices.

The bredie is an excellent kind of stew in which meat (usually lamb) and vegetables assume equal importance. Waterblommetjies, water hyacinths that grow in the dams and vleis of the Cape and taste slightly peppery, are a favourite ingredient of bredies, along with pumpkin or green vegetables.

I make my bredie with lamb and green peas, spiced with red masala paste and star anise, while doing battle with the elements and a stove which runs out of gas.

Lamb and Green Pea Bredie

Serves 4–6

100ml (4fl oz) vegetable oil

1kg (2¼lb) lamb shank, cut into steaks across the bone

3 onions, finely chopped

1 teaspoon star anise

1 tablespoon red masala curry paste

5 green chillies, chopped

5 garlic cloves, roughly chopped

3 sprigs of fresh thyme

1 litre (1¾ pints) lamb or chicken stock

450g (1lb) potatoes, cut into large dice (or small new potatoes)

450g (1lb) fresh or frozen peas

salt and freshly ground black pepper

Heat the oil in a pan and brown the lamb. Add the onions and cook for a few minutes, then put in the star anise, red masala, chilli, garlic and thyme. Pour on the stock, cover and cook for about 20 minutes.

Add the potatoes and cook for 15–20 minutes until tender. Add the peas and cook for 5–10 minutes. Season to taste and serve with plain boiled rice and Green Apple Sambal (see below).

Green Apple Sambal

juice of 2 lemons

4 hard green apples, peeled

2 garlic cloves, crushed

2 green chillies, finely chopped

a little sugar if necessary

Put the lemon juice into a bowl and grate in the apple, tossing from time to time. Add all the remaining ingredients, adding a little sugar if you like. Mix together well.

DAY 45

BOATING

The weather is still rough, but this afternoon I valiantly sail single-handed from Rio de Janeiro to Cape Town so that Mike can get some marvellous shots of the Cape from the sea. When Sir Francis Drake rounded the Cape of Good Hope, at the foot of the peninsula, in 1580, he called it '…the most stately thing, the fairest Cape we saw in the whole circumference of the earth…' but then he wasn't pitching from one end of the galley to the other trying to prepare moules marinières.

RIGHT: Cape Town Marina

DAY 46

THE KHAYELITSHA TOWNSHIP, CAPE TOWN

The truth is that we are not yet free; we have merely achieved the freedom to be free, the right not to be oppressed. We have not taken the final step of our journey, but the first step on a longer and even more difficult road…

Nelson Mandela, *Long Walk to Freedom*

…and the men drink beer

The township stretches as far as the eye can see, a hotchpotch of corrugated tin shacks and huts made up of wooden planks and chipboard, some with roofs made from black plastic sheeting. Every so often they are interspersed with blocks of cream-coloured bungalows with red-tiled roofs. Goats roam on patches of wasteland.

Inside a small shebeen, or bar, called the Cool Spot 707, old and young men sit drinking beer and talking above the blare of pop music. The walls are a patchwork of pieces of wood, lined with cardboard. A wooden plank rests on a couple of beer crates to make

a trestle table and there is a motley selection of Formica and plastic furniture. In the dusty road outside, spindly dogs sniff about beaten-up pick-up trucks. Many of the people who have gathered to watch us set up for our cooking sketch have smeared their faces with white sunblock against the intense sunshine which today has replaced the wind and rain. Incongruously some also wear woollen hats.

Outside some of the shacks logs are piled, and here and there is a half-oil-drum braai. Many of the houses are wallpapered in a mixture of different patterns; some are plastered with newspaper; one has a wall entirely covered with wrappers from boxes of chocolate. Often the homes are only barely furnished but there are many TVs. Women cook potatoes or mealie and stew over Primus stoves.

Further into the township we find 'fast-food' stalls stacked with raw beef and sausages which will be barbecued and served wrapped in paper. A herbalist has crocodile skins, shark jaws and barks hanging inside the doorway, and a blind accordionist plays a jig, accompanied by a small boy on a makeshift drumkit, the percussion section fashioned from bottletops. Another child plays a mouth harp. Crowds gather round, singing and dancing.

Outside the 707 bar we buy a bundle of kale from a woman who carries it on her head, bound with her headscarf, and inside, amid great interest and amusement, I stir-fry it to go with my dish of pork stew and root vegetables. Apparently no one inside this all-male domain has ever seen a man cook.

Pork Stew and Greens

Serves 4–6

4 carrots, each cut into 3 pieces

5 small turnips, peeled and
  quartered

4 parsnips, cut in chunks

3 gem squash

3–4 tablespoons vegetable oil

900g (2lb) belly pork, cut into
  large chunks

2 onions, quartered

6 garlic cloves, peeled

1 teaspoon peppercorns

1 teaspoon star anise

2 bay leaves

6 cloves

1 cinnamon stick

4 sticks of celery, chopped

4 leeks, sliced

3–4 small green chillies, finely
  sliced

2 dried red chillies, chopped

1 teaspoon masala paste

3 sprigs of fresh thyme

salt

450g (1lb) kale, leaves and stalks

Parboil the carrots, turnips and parsnips and reserve about 600ml
(1 pint) of the cooking liquid. Blanch the squash.

Heat half the oil in a large pan. Add the pork and when it
begins to take on some colour add the onions, whole garlic cloves,
peppercorns, star anise, bay leaves, cloves, cinnamon, celery and
leeks. Cook, stirring frequently, until the pork is cooked – about
30 minutes. Add the fresh and dried chillies, masala and thyme,
toss well, then add the reserved vegetable stock. Season with salt
and simmer for about 20 minutes.

Add the parboiled carrots, turnips, parsnips and squash to the
pan and continue cooking until the vegetables are tender.

Meanwhile heat the remaining oil in a wok or large pan and
quickly stir-fry the kale stalks first, followed by the leaves. Season
and serve with the pork.

Cape Town and ...

...Cape Town

We drive back to the Cellars, past the stylish houses with their spacious grounds. On the terrace, surrounded by flowers, elegant, well-manicured men and women are being served drinks and elaborate plates of food. It is another South Africa. Another world.

177

DAY 47

FAIRVIEW VINEYARDS

'For connoisseurs of such things,' says wine writer John Platter in his new *South African Wine Guide*, 'the piquancy of how the new black government saved the white-owned wine farming industry from growing insolvency is exquisite.

'It took a virtual teetotalling President Nelson Mandela – and an ANC-led government with a largely non-wine drinking, beer-thirsty African constituency – to bale out wine growers, mainly Afrikaaner, mainly Nationalist Party voters who supported the twenty-seven-year incarceration of the man who opened the door to a sanctions-free, export-led wine recovery.'

We are in Paarl, in the heart of the Cape wine region, enjoying an excellent glass of Pinotage at the Fairview Estate, run by the chap John Platter has just named Wineman of the Year, Charles Back. He is a colourful character whose individual, sometimes idiosyncratic, but highly drinkable wines are doing much to bring South African winemaking, as John puts it, 'out of the shadows and into the sunshine'.

Outside the estate buildings, peacocks call and goats potter around the spiral staircase of their own rather bizarre tower. Cheese is also made on the estate, and pigs, sheep and poultry are farmed. Fairview is also home to guinea-fowl – which I am to cook against the stunning backdrop of the vineyards. I have even borrowed a Western Province rugby shirt for the occasion, and anyone who mentions the word turncoat will meet the same fate as the guinea-fowl.

If I say so myself, the guinea-fowl, cooked quite classically with lardons and bacon in a red wine and orange liqueur sauce, makes a very elegant dish, garnished with fresh thyme and segments of orange. But there is no time to hang about being self-congratulatory. There is wine to taste...

Guinea-fowl with Bacon in Wine

Serves 4

vegetable oil

450g (1lb) button onions

175g (6oz) thick bacon, cut into pieces

1 whole guinea-fowl, cut into eight (thighs, drumsticks, and halved breasts)

good splash of brandy

good splash of orange liqueur

½ bottle of red wine

50g (2oz) butter, cut into pieces

a few sprigs of fresh thyme

1 orange, cut into segments

Heat a little oil in a pan. Add the onions and cook until lightly browned and softened. Add the bacon pieces and brown. Remove from the pan and reserve. Add the guinea-fowl thighs and drumsticks and cook for a few minutes before adding the breasts. When the meat has browned pour over the brandy and flame. Add the orange liqueur and red wine and simmer for about 20 minutes until the sauce has reduced and the guinea-fowl is tender. Remove the guinea-fowl from the pan and keep warm.

Whisk the butter into the sauce until it thickens slightly and becomes shiny. Return the onions and bacon to the pan, heat through, then spoon over the guinea-fowl. Sprinkle with thyme and garnish with orange segments.

THE WINEMAKER'S TALE

Charles Back, Fairview Estate:

'My grandfather was a Lithuanian immigrant who came to this country at the turn of the century and bought two farms: first Backsberg in 1916, and then this farm in 1937. After his death in 1955, my father took over and made wine in bulk, which was sold to the KWV co-operative, where it was blended and mostly exported.

'But in 1974 we started bottling our own wine and in the last fifteen years my main focus has been on developing a style that typifies this region and Fairview. Winemaking is my obsession and my passion. To go into the cellar and try to turn out world class wine is a great challenge. Most of the estate is planted to red wine, predominantly our mainstay, Shiraz, backed up with Merlot, Cabernet Sauvignon, Malbec and one or two other Rhône varieties such as Mourvedre. I am very much a Rhône fan. In the white wines we plant predominantly Chardonnay, Sauvignon Blanc, Viognier (another Rhône grape) and Semillon, which has done particularly well this year.

'Seventy-five per cent of the wine is sold in the UK, and our styles have been greatly influenced by what I've seen in Australia, California and obviously France. I brought all the ideas home, put them in a pot, stirred them round with a bit of African flavour and came up with something I think is identifiably Fairview. The style is not as overtly fruit-driven as some winemakers in the New World try to make; we try to marry the fruit-driven style with more traditional European styles.

'Right now South Africa is a very exciting place to be. We have to redefine our place in the world. Thirty years ago South African winemakers were New World leaders. They felt they had found their niche. They thought they were world-beaters and they were complacent and self-assured. Then we went into the isolation period and came out the other end still expecting to be champs. I've never had that attitude. I looked at things the other way round. I knew we had fallen way behind and that we had serious work to do. But it has been a bit of a shock to many to discover that we have to re-establish ourselves. People have had to go back to the drawing-board very quickly.

'But South Africans as a whole have an ability to adapt quickly. On the political front that is quite evident. And on the wine front we had the resources, the technology and 300 years of winemaking skills. And the sense to realize that we had to change. That is what is happening in the South African wine industry at the moment with dramatic results.

'There is no other place in the world like this for growing grapes. In terms of natural resources we are world class and that is going to be demonstrated. We have the climate, and the Cape Doctor which blows all the disease away, giving us healthy fruit which is almost table-grape quality in appearance. And healthy fruit means that we can reduce the SO_2 levels in the wine, which is going to be a major factor.

'The decks are stacked in our favour. As we showed with our rugby, we are going to be right back there on top. I promise you.'

Spectacular colours of Africa

DAY 48

ON THE ROAD AGAIN

A wild wind whips around the waterfront, pricking the skin with particles of sand and hurling tables and chairs from restaurant patios. In the bay huge breakers peak in an angry sea under a dense cloud of spray and a fire in the hillside sends orange smoke billowing out over the water.

I leave the city in its strange, ugly mood. Tomorrow we fly to Bloemfontein. From there we will drive to the mountain kingdom of Lesotho.

As the Range Rover gathers speed I reflect on the fact that throughout my journey in Africa people have repeatedly said to me, with gushing enthusiasm: 'Just wait until you get to Cape Town…', but as the city falls away into the distance behind me, I am still not quite sure why.

DAY 49

MASERU

There are fourteen border posts leading to Lesotho. From Bloemfontein we cross at Maseru Bridge, which carries a plaque proclaiming it to be the winner of the Border Post Competition for 1978. From here it is only a few miles to the capital, Maseru, whose name refers to the rich red sandstone which surrounds the sprawling city.

They call Lesotho the kingdom in the sky. The peaks of the Maluti mountains exceed 3,000 metres, and in winter they are capped with snow. Since part of the wild mountain terrain is still inaccessible to vehicles, the horse remains an essential mode of transport for the Basotho people whose origins lie with the Tswana tribes of Botswana. Long, long ago they made the trek to this mountainous country, which gained its independence in 1966.

RIGHT: Lesotho horseman in traditional hat and cape

DAY 50

COMES A HORSEMAN

The outskirts of Maseru straggle on. Dilapidated buses and pick-up trucks lie abandoned by the roadside in front of garages, general stores and clothing depots. Rows of low stone houses stretch into the distance. Roadside stalls hold neat but meagre piles of oranges, tomatoes and greens.

Slowly the city gives way to green meadows where maize grows in the orange-red earth. Herdsmen carrying staffs and wrapped in traditional patterned blankets amble past with their flocks of sheep and goats and herds of cows. Here and there donkeys, but mostly horses, graze; some freely, some tethered. The Basotho horse is a sturdy, pretty breed, a mix of Javanese pony, English thoroughbred and the Dutch-descended Boer horse.

The stone houses are fewer now and the familiar African round mud huts with their thatched roofs cluster together. We pass tractors and lorries with their trailers filled with workers; donkeys carry sacks and oxen pull carts.

Ahead are the mountains, their rocky crowns sculpted into craggy faces. Their green hillsides, peppered with enormous boulders and soft grey aloe plants, have a wild, welcoming beauty.

We turn off the surprisingly good tarmacked road and climb towards the Royal Village of Matsieng, second home of King Moshoeshoe II and Queen 'M'e Mamohato. Today I am to cook for the Queen.

Down the hillside ahead of us, their hooves stirring up the red dust, come four riders, flying like proud Horsemen of the Apocalypse, resplendent in their coloured blankets and the famous wide-brimmed conical straw hats, said to be modelled on the shape of many of the kingdom's mountains. One of the riders has the reins to a fifth horse, saddled and bridled. I am to make the final part of the journey on horseback.

My sure-footed mount makes his confident way over the stony hillside, through charming clusters of thatched mud huts whose quaintly painted window frames and doors give them the look of fairy dwellings from a child's story book.

The royal residence is set back from the village. A low bungalow with a beautifully kept lawn and beds of roses, geraniums, marigolds and pansies, it would not be out of place in an English coastal town.

Through a gate in a bamboo fence, with lintels bound by exquisitely worked plaited and twisted grass, women with blankets tied around their waists sit plucking chickens. Chicken farming is an integral part of the royal estate and in Lesotho as a whole, and a brand new chicken house is being built next to the stables. The chickens are slaughtered outside the bamboo fence, then washed and dipped into boiling water to make their feathers easier to pull. On a fire next to the vat of boiling water an enormous black pot of yellow mealie is being stirred into a thick porridge by an elderly woman. Lunch for the workers.

RIGHT: Plucking chickens

The Basotho people are known for their friendliness towards strangers and we are made hugely welcome. The younger children frolic over the rocky hillsides as surefootedly as goats, some playing with ingenious toys fashioned from wire. The older children will return from school later.

Among the attractive houses I cook my royal meal of chicken kebabs with corn fritters, spicy tomato sauce and pineapple, ginger and chilli salad. Her Majesty, a charming lady with a keen interest in cooking, has prepared some dishes for me to try: fat cakes (like beignets), traditional Basotho corn fritters, and bowls of pounded wheat and peas, cooked with spices. There is also steamed bread. Ovens are rare here, so the loaves are put into small pots inside cooking pots filled with boiling water and left to steam over an open fire. The food is quite delicious.

Fortunately the Queen is equally gracious in her praise for my dishes and tucks in wholeheartedly. It seems she particularly likes my hot tomato sauce. I am granted permission to stay in the kingdom.

Pineapple, Ginger and Chilli Salad

½ fresh pineapple, cut into
   chunks
25g (1oz) fresh root ginger,
   chopped

2 green chillies, chopped
½ a cucumber, cut into same size
   chunks as the pineapple
2 tablespoons white wine vinegar

Mix together all the ingredients and leave to marinate for at least
15 minutes.

The Queen and I…

Royal Kebabs with Corn Fritters and Spicy Tomato Sauce

Serves 4

4 boneless chicken breasts, cubed

For the Marinade
250ml (9fl oz) olive oil
1 onion, chopped
1 tablespoon fresh thyme leaves
1 tablespoon piri piri sauce
   (available from specialist
   grocers and delicatessens)

For the Tomato Sauce
2 tablespoons olive oil
1 onion, thinly sliced
2 garlic cloves
1 x approx. 400g (14oz) tin
   tomatoes, chopped and juice
   reserved
2 sprigs of fresh thyme

2 red chillies
salt

For the Corn Fritters
100g (4oz) butter
100g (4oz) flour
300ml (½ pint) milk
150g (5oz) sweetcorn
1 red chilli, seeded and chopped
1 green chilli, seeded and chopped
1 teaspoon finely chopped fresh
   root ginger
1 garlic clove, chopped
1 tablespoon chopped celery
   leaves
salt
flour for dredging

Mix together the marinade ingredients and add the chicken. Marinate for at least 2 hours.

To make the tomato sauce, heat the oil in a wok or large pan, add the onion and cook gently until it begins to colour. Add the garlic and cook for a minute or so. Add the tomatoes, thyme and chillies and season with salt. Simmer for about 20 minutes.

To make the corn fritters, melt the butter in a pan, stir in the flour and cook gently for 1–2 minutes. Stir in the milk gradually and cook until you have a very thick paste. Mix in the sweetcorn, chillies, ginger, garlic, celery and salt. Cool slightly, then form into round cakes and dredge with flour. Heat some oil in a pan and gently fry the fritters for about 5 minutes on each side, until golden.

Meanwhile thread the chicken on to skewers and grill or barbecue, turning often, for 10–15 minutes. Serve with the corn fritters and spicy tomato sauce, plus some salad (see page 197).

DAY 51

THE MALUTI MOUNTAINS

A strange procession makes its way through the mountains: me, Mike and the film crew, carrying assorted pieces of equipment, astride donkeys. This is the only way we can reach the particular spot we have chosen for today's cooking sketch, in the mountains above the Royal Village. At first the journey is as comfortable as can be expected on board a bony donkey, but when the track narrows to a few inches around the edge of the mountains I can't begin to look down.

The donkeys, however, have trodden the path a hundred times before and we are delivered safely. Women without the luxury of such transport wind their way higher through the mountain pass to the next village, carrying their bundles on their heads. A young boy on horseback gallops after them, dust and stones flying.

Amid sand-coloured boulders and aloe plants I fry mealie balls stuffed with spicy pork and tomatoes. The villagers who have followed us up the mountain cluster round, some holding brightly coloured parasols against the fierce sun. A woman takes snuff from a small box. The people are fascinated and eager to taste the food. Like their Queen, they love spicy food, but the spices are hard to come by.

As the sun begins to set the mountains blush deep pink. We take our farewells and the children flock around waving and smiling. With reluctance we leave this pretty, welcoming place.

Deep-fried Spicy Mealie Balls

Serves 4

450g (1lb) mealie (maize flour, from health food shops)
4 tablespoons vegetable oil
salt
pinch of cayenne pepper
275g (10oz) lean pork, cut into small dice
1 onion, chopped
2 garlic cloves, crushed
1 teaspoon crushed fresh root ginger
1 sprig of thyme
3 tomatoes, skinned, seeded and diced
2 green chillies, chopped
biryani curry powder, to taste
150g (5oz) diced dried fruit (apricot, pear, plum, apple, etc.)
flour for dredging
oil for deep frying

Mix the mealie with 2 tablespoons of the vegetable oil, salt, cayenne pepper and a little water and cook until you have the consistency of firm mashed potato.

Heat the remaining 2 tablespoons of oil in a pan, add the pork and cook briefly to brown, then add the onion, garlic, ginger and thyme and cook for a few minutes. Add the tomatoes, chillies and curry powder and simmer for about 15 minutes. Stir in the dried fruit. Leave to cool slightly before mixing into the mealie.

Form the mixture into little balls, dredge with flour, then deep fry in oil until golden. Serve with Achard (see page 88), to which a little sliced green mango has been added.

DAY 52

THE ROOF OF AFRICA RALLY

A small contretemps is going on between the Floyd crew and the officials of the Roof of Africa Rally. The streets of Maseru are crowded with spectators and lined with flags and bunting for the Round the Houses race. Traditionally today's race launches the annual rally, a spectacular 1,000 kilometre slide, bump and scramble through rough terrain, rivers and mud in the Maluti mountains.

Though we have cleared the arrangements with the organizers in advance, the race officials are unhappy about my cooking on a braai on a dangerous corner as the off-road vehicles, with their specially strengthened bodies and high wheels, hurtle past. They are afraid I will cause an inferno if one of them crashes into me.

A very large, determined-looking lady heads my way to explain her position. I send in Stan. After a moment's negotiation, I move back an inch or so and the race is on.

From the Basotho Hat craft centre on the same corner the race commentator simultaneously gives updates on the race and on the state of the lamb chops, steaks and boerewors on my braai. Hoarse from shouting over the noise of the engines, I pour myself a whisky to lubricate the throat, and settle back to watch the next race. Could that really be Stan taking the corner on two wheels in a converted Range Rover?

DAY 53

JOHANNESBURG AIRPORT

Chocks away. The noise from the Pratt & Whitney engines of the Junkers 52 is deafening as slowly, slowly, at a speed of about 100 kilometres per hour, the fabulous black and silver flying machine takes off on huge fat wheels from an airstrip at Jan Smuts airport (named after the former prime minister). Captain Brian Stableford suggests that windows should be wound down with care, as objects might fly out and annoy people on the ground.

In the brown and cream interior with its 'string-bag' luggage rack, a tall air hostess whose head almost touches the ceiling serves soft drinks. Through the open cockpit I see dials and levers with coloured knobs and wooden wheels. There are three people flying the plane: the pilot, the co-pilot and a flight engineer.

The JU52s were the backbone of the Luftwaffe and the South African Airforce during the war. This aircraft, called Jan van Riebeeck after the Dutchman who led the first expedition to the Cape in 1652, was the fourth last to be built under licence in Spain in 1954. Now it is being used for charters by South African Airlines.

It has been a Jan Smuts kind of day. This morning, having moaned once too often about airline food, South African Airlines challenged me to cook my idea of a good airline meal, under the watchful eye of Ian Kehoe, executive chef of the Holiday Inn at Jan Smuts. Ten years ago Ian was in charge of preparing up to 5,000 first class meals every day for airlines such as British Airways, Lufthansa and Swissair.

Since I always crave spicy food when I am flying, I made a tangy little stir-fried number with pork fillet, peppers, ginger, garlic and black bean sauce, and served it with a Haute Cabrière Estate blend of Chardonnay and Pinot Noir.

Vintage Junkers

Now I am cruising at about 1,000 feet at a speed of about 185 kilometres per hour and with every spot of turbulence the stomach lurches. Below, the city of Johannesburg is clearly defined by avenues of jacaranda trees. It is an exhilarating trip, a reminder of what real flying used to be about. I suggested bringing my gas-fired wok to cook on board but they wouldn't let me, so instead I settle back and enjoy the flight to... well, I'll have to watch the programme to find that one out.

Soweto

DAY 54

SOWETO

The road to Soweto (short for South Western Townships) leads through Houghton, one of Johannesburg's most attractive suburbs, with its big houses, lavish gardens and profusion of purple jacaranda.

As we drive on, we leave the skyscrapers and sleek mirrored buildings behind. The skyline could be that of any major American city.

Ahead are the painted hoardings and barbed-wire-topped walls so familiar from television news bulletins. Soweto stretches ahead into the distance. The township is as large as the city of Birmingham.

We pass clinics, a maternity ward and cheerful cafés in corrugated metal shacks. A barricade of old buses, painted jauntily with fruit and vegetables, serves as a market, the insides of the vehicles stacked out with produce and sacks of grain. Nearby, sheep are herded into pens for sale. Past the Vista University and the football stadium are neat brick bungalows, but rubbish litters the wasteground which separates them from the road. A brick and tile yard carries the slogan: 'We Build the New South Africa Better'.

We stop at a fruit and vegetable market, where the quality of the produce is some of the best we have seen on any stalls so far in Africa. There are piles of onions, cabbages, bananas, greens, pineapples. Across the road a low block of stores sells everything from hardware and electrical goods to bicycles, wool and toiletries.

Past a golf course created on rough ground, we drive on through the mixture of brick houses and shacks and pull up alongside a church. A trailer carrying Sunday School children pulls up. They are dressed in costumes for a pageant. From inside the church comes the sound of singing. In the distance sirens scream.

Behind the church is a community centre. Inside is the Food Gardens Foundation, where usually a lady called Phyllis from the Black Women's League teaches the basics of cooking and baking. But today I am to cook for a group of students who intend to carve out careers for themselves in the food business.

RIGHT: Market in Soweto

Behind the kitchen is the garden run by Grace Mashigo, which supplies much of the produce for Phyllis's cooking sessions. Her mission is to help ease the problem of poverty in Soweto by teaching people to be self-sufficient, even in the average 'door-sized' garden. In the deceptively arid ground neatly planted beds of herbs are labelled with suggested uses, a profusion of vegetables, such as celery, beans, onions, spinach, peppers and chillies are packed into spaces under windows or along fences, and

potatoes are grown in rubber tyres. Everything is designed to show the potential of even the tiniest plot.

Since there is a strong Portuguese influence in Johannesburg I am cooking a Cataplana, made with pork and seafood. The students are a smart bunch who keep me on my toes and ask pertinent questions, but tellingly, one of their main concerns is how much such a dish might cost to make.

DAY 55

THE ROAD TO SUN CITY

Stalls selling pottery, rugs, silk paintings and wooden carved animals line the road from Johannesburg. We pass platinum mines and the now-familiar tin shack settlements. Ahead the arid, rocky slopes of the mountains are covered with scrubby bushes, like stubble. After about an hour and a half of driving through the hot, dry landscape, we turn through a big stone gate into the South African playground of Sun City in the former independent state of Bophuthatswana.

The lost palace

DAYS 55, 56, 57

THE LOST CITY

The report of the treasure went down indeed among the people who lived in the country from age to age, but none knew where the chamber was, nor the secret of the door. But it happened that a white man reached this country from over the mountains…
H. Rider Haggard, *King Solomon's Mines*

The days and nights roll into one in the bizarre fantastical pleasure kingdom of Sun City. According to legend, long, long ago a people from North Africa journeyed south and built a magnificent metropolis in the volcanic crater they called the Valley of the Sun. But it was destroyed in an almighty earthquake and for centuries explorers spoke of finding the Lost City.

Four years ago the multi-millionaire Sol Kerzner, the man behind the casino-resort of Sun City, 'discovered' it at a cost of around $276 million. At the centre of it all is the Palace. With its towers and domes, it is a riot of columns, mosaics and marble, palm trees and crystal chandeliers, gigantic bronze sculptures of elephant, leopard and leaping buck and cheetah, and stone passages lit by flames. Beyond, there is a jungle, a rain forest, an amphitheatre, ancient ruins and a bridge that shudders with mock earthquakes. In the Valley of the Waves there are terrifying water shutes and surf-sized waves, and in the Pilanesberg National Park next door, the Big Five (lion, leopard, elephant, rhino and buffalo) roam, along with giraffe, zebra, wildebeest and springbok. There is even a cinema, where they are showing Alan Paton's heartrending story of Apartheid, *Cry the Beloved Country*.

As we film, we follow in the footsteps of other crews, recording other dramas. Every now and then we bump into sinister-looking characters in long robes on the set of *Peanuts, The Movie*.

Fact and fantasy begin to blur together in a most confusing way. Only in the small hours when the last revellers pit themselves

against fate in the casino, and an army of workers swarms into the Palace to polish the vast expanses of glass and remove the plants for watering, do you remember that it is all a show.

But there is one very real person in Sun City: executive chef Toni Robertson, a tiny lady who has trodden the road from Mandalay to the Lost City with steely determination and whose razor-sharp instincts for good food have won quite a reputation for the cuisine at the Palace's Crystal Court restaurant. Born in Burma, she worked in France and Chicago before Sun City's food supremo John Makin brought her to the Lost City.

Together we prepare three dishes that typify her passion for flavourful food impregnated with tastes and ideas from all over the world. Many of the ingredients are freshly picked from her huge vegetable and herb garden just outside the gates of the City.

The first dish is Cape Malay crayfish, a fabulous concoction of pan-fried crayfish marinated in chilli, ginger and lemon grass, served with spicy fried rice and tomato chutney and topped with her trademark deep-fried, caramelized 'tobacco' onions and a poached egg. The second is ostrich hash, in which South Africa meets West Coast America, and finally there is a mixed grill of fish, with vegetables and pesto mashed potatoes, spiced up with that wonderful tomato chutney.

LEFT: And all in the best possible taste

Cape Malay Crayfish with Fried Rice and Sesame Chopsticks

Serves 4

2 whole crayfish or lobster, halved

2 crayfish or lobster, chopped

2 onions, chopped

oil for shallow and deep frying

1 small bunch of spring onions, chopped

100g (4oz) beanshoots

1 green chilli, chopped

1 red chilli, chopped

25g (1oz) fresh root ginger, chopped

1 garlic clove, chopped

4 spears of asparagus, chopped

225g (8oz) long-grain white rice, cooked

100g (4oz) chopped pineapple

2 tablespoons cashew nuts

3 tablespoons soy sauce

3 tablespoons oyster sauce

4 eggs

For the Tomato Chutney

6 tomatoes, peeled, seeded and diced

½ a papaya, diced

2 teaspoons tomato ketchup

2 teaspoons balsamic vinegar

pinch of sugar

1 garlic clove, chopped

1 red chilli, chopped

1 green chilli, chopped

For the Sesame Chopsticks

8 spring roll skins

2 egg yolks, beaten

2 tablespoons sesame seeds

For the Marinade

150ml (5fl oz) groundnut oil

2 stalks of lemon grass, outer leaves removed, bruised

25g (1oz) fresh root ginger, finely chopped

2 garlic cloves, chopped

1 red chilli, chopped

1 green chilli, chopped

small bunch of fresh chives

For the Julienne of Raw Vegetables

1 red pepper, cut into julienne strips

1 stick of celery, cut into julienne strips

1 carrot, cut into julienne strips

1 courgette, cut into julienne strips

Combine all the ingredients for the tomato chutney and reserve. Brush the spring roll skins with egg yolk, roll in the sesame seeds, then roll up to resemble chopsticks. Deep-fry and reserve. Combine the marinade ingredients, and marinate the halved crayfish in this mixture for about 2 hours. Deep-fry the onions until golden and crispy. Reserve.

Heat some oil in a pan until it is smoking. Put in the halved crayfish and cook hard for a few minutes on each side. Meanwhile heat a little more oil in a wok and quickly stir-fry the chopped crayfish for a minute or two, add the spring onions and stir-fry for a further minute or two, then add the beanshoots, chillies, ginger and garlic and stir-fry for another minute. Add the chopped asparagus, followed by the rice, and finally the pineapple and cashew nuts. Splash in the soy sauce and oyster sauce, toss well and divide between 4 warm plates.

Quickly fry the eggs and place one on top of each mound of rice and vegetables, followed by a handful of the julienne of vegetables. Top this with the fried onions and place the crayfish on top. Garnish each plate with 2 sesame chopsticks and serve with the tomato chutney.

Ostrich Hash

The term hash is not strictly correct, because the finished dish does not form a cake – rather it is a mixture that is piled up. Editor, please note, once again you could substitute fillet steak for ostrich.

Serves 4

butter

225g (8oz) ostrich fillet, diced

salt and freshly ground black
  pepper

small bunch of spring onions,
  chopped

225g (8oz) potatoes, diced and
  parboiled

100g (4oz) pumpkin, diced and
  parboiled

1 red pepper, diced and blanched

1 green pepper, diced and
  blanched

1 yellow pepper, diced and
  blanched

4 eggs

For the Hollandaise Sauce

juice of 1 lemon

juice of 1 orange

juice of 1 grapefruit

2 egg yolks

275g (10oz) warm clarified butter

For the Garnish

1 orange, cut into segments

1 lemon, cut into segments

1 pink grapefruit, cut into
  segments

Heat a little butter in a pan and sauté the diced ostrich. Season, then add the spring onions, potatoes, pumpkin and peppers and cook for about 5 minutes, stirring frequently.

Meanwhile make the hollandaise sauce. First put the fruit juices into a pan, bring to the boil and reduce by half. Put into a large heatproof bowl with the egg yolks and whisk over a pan of hot water until frothy. Dribble in the butter very slowly, whisking continuously until it is thick and creamy (if it becomes too thick, add a drop of water).

Poach the eggs. To serve, pile the ostrich hash on to 4 warm plates, top each with a poached egg and a little hollandaise sauce, and garnish with orange, lemon and grapefruit segments.

Mixed Grill of Fish

You could substitute monkfish for kingclip in this recipe.

Serves 4

2 red peppers, halved

2 green peppers, halved

vegetable oil

12 asparagus tips

12 baby sweetcorn

12 oyster mushrooms

4 baby yellow courgettes, halved
lengthways

450g (1lb) kingclip or monkfish

450g (1lb) salmon

12 prawns

12 mussels, scrubbed

6 large potatoes, cooked and
mashed

2 tablespoons pesto sauce

For the Herb Vinaigrette

300ml (½ pint) olive oil

1 carrot, finely diced

1 red pepper, finely diced

1 green pepper, finely diced

6 shallots, finely chopped

3 garlic cloves, finely chopped

a little red wine vinegar, to taste

1 tablespoon chopped mixed
fresh thyme, basil and oregano

salt and freshly ground black
pepper

Mix together the ingredients for the vinaigrette. Peel the peppers by grilling them, skin side uppermost, until they blister. Cover with a damp cloth and leave to cool, then peel and quarter. Heat a little oil in a pan, put in the peppers and cook until they begin to soften. Turn up the heat and add the rest of the vegetables, except for the mashed potato. Cook, stirring frequently for a few minutes, until the vegetables are just soft.

Brush the fish with oil and grill (salmon and kingclip or monkfish first, followed by the prawns and mussels). Heat the mashed potato and mix in the pesto. To serve put a little pesto mash on to 4 warmed plates, prop the fish and vegetables all around, top with the prawns and mussels, and spoon over the vinaigrette. Serve with tomato chutney (see pages 214–15).

THE CHEF'S TALE

Toni Robertson, executive chef of the Palace, came to Sun City in 1994.

'Even as a child in Burma I always wanted to be in the kitchen – though I was a nurse in the US Airforce before I took up cooking as a career. When John Makin brought me to see the Lost City and the Palace I fell in love with it. I couldn't believe this building. I went straight home and packed my bags. I saw this as a real opportunity to work with the local Tswana people and put my thumbprint on the food here.

'What I try to do is produce simple elegant food, using traditional South African ingredients, but with influences from around the world. After all what is South African cooking? It is full of Dutch influences, British, Cape Malay, Portuguese...Or it is the simple food of the local people: mealie pap and stew.

'I have worked in Paris and Chicago and Beverly Hills but you always go back to your roots – a noodle soup your grandmother made or a special meal your parents prepared – so the Asian influence is very strong in my cooking.

'I love to experiment and have fun with food, but I'm not crazy like a lot of chefs who want to use all the ingredients they have discovered in one dish. I believe above all that chicken should taste like chicken and fish should taste like fish.'

DAY 58

THE LOST CITY

The sun is going down over the wave pool. Toni Robertson and her kitchen team have piled a table high with meats and fish for the braai, spicy noodle and rice salads, luscious tropical fruits and delicate petits fours. It is our last cooking sketch of the series, and it will turn into the crew party. As the champagne corks pop we are joined by five leggy hopefuls from the Miss World Contest, which is held here each year. They nibble and sip prettily before they are whisked away to their next engagement, a trail of photographers following in their wake.

Miss Worlds and me

One by one the last bathers pick up their belongings. The wave machine is still and the sun begins to set softly over the beach. The fairground has closed and the people have gone home. But the lights are starting to glitter in the Palace. For other adventurers the evening's entertainment is about to begin.

In the quiet of the gathering darkness I remember another Africa: music in the shebeen in a Cape Town township, happy children frolicking with goats and wire toys in the Lesotho hillside, women feeding their babies inside thatched mud huts and sunshine on a Madagascar paddy-field. I remember an elephant called Hector, and the chilling stare of a lion, almost camouflaged in the buff-coloured bush. I put out the stove and pick up my hat. It is time to go home.

INDEX